BOOKS BY

MARION L. STARKEY

A LITTLE REBELLION

(*1955*)

THE DEVIL IN MASSACHUSETTS

(*1949*)

THE CHEROKEE NATION

(*1946*)

These are BORZOI BOOKS
published in New York by ALFRED A. KNOPF

A LITTLE REBELLION

A Little Rebellion

BY

MARION L. STARKEY

New York

ALFRED·A·KNOPF

1955

L. C. catalog card number: 55-9292

© *Marion L. Starkey, 1955*

THIS IS A BORZOI BOOK,
PUBLISHED BY ALFRED A. KNOPF, INC.

FIRST EDITION

FOR

L. L. W.

"I hold it that a little rebellion now and then is a good thing, and as necessary in the political world as storms in the physical.... The tree of liberty must be refreshed from time to time with the blood of patriots and tyrants. It is its natural manure."

—THOMAS JEFFERSON
apropos of Daniel Shays in Massachusetts

ACKNOWLEDGMENTS

M<small>Y</small> <small>THANKS TO</small> the many kind people in assorted libraries and archives — and one jail — who helped me in my research.

These include the entire staff of the Massachusetts Archives at the State House in Boston; many of the staff of the Boston Athenaeum, the Massachusetts Historical Society, the Boston Public Library, the Records of the Massachusetts Supreme Judicial Court, the Old State House in Boston, the Widener Library at Harvard University, the Library of the College of Liberal Arts at Boston University, the Forbes Library in Northampton, the Hampshire County Courthouse, the Berkshire Athenaeum in Pittsfield, the Manuscript Room in the New York Public Library, the National Archives and the Congressional Library in Washington, the Vermont Historical Society in Montpelier, Vermont.

The jail is the House of Correction in Northampton, whose attendants, rummaging in the vaults, discovered for me forgotten jail and debtors'-prison records kept at the time of Shays' Rebellion.

My thanks to farmers in and about Williamstown, Vermont, who sketched out for me the details of old-time farm life and the enduring nature of farm problems, and gave me points on how they would have behaved if they had been faced with the problems that roused Daniel Shays; to those people of Pelham, Massachusetts, who talked over with me the traditions of Shays (they are proud of him) and the special difficulties of farming in the Pelham hills; to the Trailways bus-drivers who obligingly picked me up and put me down at unscheduled stops in Shays country.

Now to particularize.

Everyone who works in the Massachusetts Archives gets help amounting to collaboration from Leo Flaherty, Senior Archives Assistant, who not only knows his records, but has the ingenuity of Detective Sergeant Friday in running down an obscure source.

Sidney Kaplan of the University of Massachusetts, himself the author of many valuable monographs on Shays' Rebellion, generously opened his massive notes to me; Dr. Robert E. Moody, of Boston University, was always available for a consultation; Frank W. Grinnell, secretary of the Massachusetts Bar Association, gave me materials and advice on legal problems; Joseph B. Berry — usually consulted at that charming institution, tea at the Boston Athenaeum — either knew the answer to every historical conundrum that perplexed me or the most likely source in which to seek it. W. Kay Lamb, Dominion Archivist at the Public Archives of Canada, checked for me the record of Shays' flight to Canada. Mrs. William L. Tisdel dug up the records of Shays' residence in New York State and took me on a grand tour of Shays country; Mrs. Harvey L. Gray guided us to historical points of the Springfield area; Mrs. William A. Berridge to the battlefield in lovely South Egremont. Mrs. Florence S. Cummings entrusted me with relevant details from her own historical collections.

I am grateful to the John Simon Guggenheim Memorial Foundation for making it possible for me to have a free year for my research, and to the University of Connecticut for giving me time off for the purpose. I am indebted to my editor, Harold Strauss, for his patience in helping me shape an exceedingly rough first draft into more graceful form; to Laurence L. Winship of the *Boston Globe,* who also read the manuscript at its most awkward stage and gave sound advice on its reconstruction.

I am indebted for all manner of aid and comfort to Bernard and Avis De Voto, to Malcolm S. and Marion MacLean, to E. A. Laycock, August Heckscher, John K. Hutchens, to Francis and Lillian Irons, to Dr. Odell Shepard, Dr. Donald Derby, William Towner, and Dorothy Canfield Fisher.

And I owe not the least to the friend who gave me loyal companionship during the long and lonely task of writing, my cat Cherokee.

CONTENTS

Contents

A LITTLE REBELLION

"*Unterribly in Massachusetts*"

Since it is no secret that wars and revolutions seldom settle anything, the founding fathers of the republic should have been less startled than they were when shortly after the close of the American Revolution, in Massachusetts the minutemen marched again.

It happened in 1786. For the second time in a decade, the conch shells sounded on the village greens and the minutemen marched; they were not only animated by the same spirit that had impelled them on the road to Lexington, but many of them were the same men. They were supported by much of the old revolutionary paraphernalia: county conventions, committees of correspondence, resolutions solemnly taken. But this time they marched without the blessing of Boston, which in their eyes had replaced Britain as the Enemy. And they did not have the old leadership. Those men who so short a time ago had assured them that such conduct was logical, virtuous, and nobly patriotic now looked on aghast. George Washington wrung his hands and faced the fact that his dream of retiring to the placid obscurity of a country gentleman was premature; unfinished business demanded his attention. Sam Adams, who so recently had been at such pains to rouse them to a proper revolutionary pitch, looked on ·

3

with something of the affront of an impresario who sees his epic production plagiarized by amateurs and received by the gross masses with even more enthusiasm than the original had been.

Of all the leaders of the earlier revolution, only Thomas Jefferson expressed anything like approval. "A little rebellion now and then," he remarked, is a good thing for a republic; but Jefferson, being in Paris, was at too far a remove to influence the course of events. The "rebels" never even heard that he was for them.

Those of the founding fathers who were closer to the event, particularly authorities in Massachusetts, believed that a government which must be sparked by a series of rebellions, little or otherwise, is no better than anarchy. Accordingly, they set out to suppress this one. In their fright they were perhaps not entirely intelligent about it; careful scrutiny of the conduct of our illustrious fore-fathers sometimes gives grounds for suspicion that they were not always much brighter than we are. Thanks largely to a certain obtuseness in their outlook, what at first could be dismissed as mere "commotions" presently had to be recognized as "rebellion," and finally the harassed commonwealth of Massachusetts declared itself in a "state of war."

It wasn't a long war. The rebels, as confused, as divided in their thinking as their political betters, ill equipped and clumsily led, endowed by no ideology more fanatic than what they found in Scripture and in Mr. Jefferson's Declaration, were in no position to defeat Boston.

Nor was it a bloody war. A latter-day Massachusetts slaughters more on its roads on a fine week-end than did the armies of Captain Daniel Shays and General Benjamin Lincoln in all the battlegrounds of a winter's campaign. The rebels themselves carried their muskets for months without firing a shot; never were so many village Hampdens so guiltless of their country's blood. Nor could the government be called murderous; true, the cry of murder was raised against it when in a crisis it cut loose with its howitzers; but once it got the upper hand, it was singularly indisposed to demonstrate the majesty of the law on the gibbet. Only two "rebels" ever did hang — to their vast and touching bewilderment — and this for special cause not directly connected with rebellion.

A rebellion that results in few killings, no hangings, except for the hapless pair who were not rebels only, offers little to the injustice-collectors of the major ideologies, for all that what came to be called Shays' Rebellion did bear some resemblance to a class war. Even to construct high tragedy from the episode requires the medium of fiction rather than of history. The rebels were simple people, little given to putting their private griefs on paper and, even if they had done so, not the sort whose papers get preserved from generation to generation and presently handed over to the historical societies. It is as hard to get at their intimate histories as if they were not men of good Puritan stock but so many wild Indians. Like most Indians, their history is recorded by their enemies. Luckily, the latter were compassionate more often than not, and sometimes perceptive. Even so, it would be hard to make an Orestes or an Œdipus of the rebel most thoroughly put on record, Captain Shays.

But the little rebellion had consequences. No event which calls a Washington back to public life, sets the best minds of the nation to re-examining their political philosophy, and impels thirteen governments of violently divergent interest into adopting "a more perfect union," can be dismissed as without effect. Not that the constitution of the United States was an aim of the rebels; on the contrary, they did their best to head it off; it became, however, one of their involuntary achievements.

The western world today is in a condition not unlike that of America in the years immediately following the Revolution. The scale is immensely larger, the conflicts tragically intensified, the ideologies set on a more rigid pattern, yet an analogy is there. We too suffer blank misgivings of a creature moving in worlds not realized; we too, owing immediate allegiance to governments of divergent interests, are fumbling our way to a notion of a larger entity above and beyond them, to the concept of a "natural law" under which all men can rationally govern themselves. We are still beset with the problem of how to make democracy work, and in our insecurities are still tempted to ascribe all our troubles to our enemies instead of finding the cause of some of them in our own imperfections. For the world at large the same problems that sent Massachusetts farmers down the road to rebellion are still unsolved, and for all our century and a half of experience we are not visibly more intelligent than our ancestors.

Implausible to hope that we can solve our problems with as little bloodletting as did Massachusetts in 1787 when so much has been let already. Yet it is instructive to note that if the crisis of 1786 passed unterribly in Massachusetts partly because of God's grace and sheer good luck, it was also because in both factions, men of good sense and good will outnumbered the fanatics. In our brutal age their story may seem insignificant and lacking in drama. But does it take a blood bath and hangings to produce drama? Surely if the world is to be civilized, and civilization is to be sane, it is better not to hang or get hanged; and if the reason for the omission can be found in the gentleness and wisdom of men, examination of these qualities is of greater moment than studies in sadism.

CHAPTER I

The Conventions

ʬʬʬ

Rebellion was in the making in Massachusetts in the *I* spring of 1786. Not that it started as one. Rebellion as such was the last thing any responsible man wanted, and the prospective rebels, the hard-pressed farmers of the western counties, were God-fearing, responsible men.

They stayed with due process of the law as long as they *II* could. In the spring they did nothing more subversive than assemble in town meeting to petition Legislature for relief from their burdens. Some of the petitions might be adjudged somewhat subversive in content, but not even Boston could deny their right to make them.

In the summer, at least from early June to July 8, while Legislature sat, the farmers waited quietly to see what it could accomplish for them. That it accomplished little was, however, in part their own fault. Perversely, in this *III* calamitous year many of the towns most clamorous for relief failed in their duty of sending a representative to General Court, as the Legislature was called. In the "outer counties" — that is, all those west of Boston: Middlesex, Worcester, Hampshire, Berkshire — as many as fifty per cent of the towns had sent no delegates. Thus, when their ally in the east, Bristol County, on the border of what Boston called "Rogue's Island," pushed a bill dear to the

Reason quasi unresponsive to needs of the unrepresented

7

hearts of the farmers, a measure providing for paper
money, it did not pass. Nor could all the efforts of such
western delegates as were present block measures that
seemed to them designed to hike the intolerable burden
of debts and taxes still further.

"Mr. Speaker, this measure will never do!" western
delegates shouted hoarsely. "The *People,* sir, will never
bear it. The measure is determined against their will."

But they shouted in vain. When in July Governor James
Bowdoin turned them out to pasture, the upcountry delegates went home to report that General Court had given
them stone who had asked for bread.

"The General Court are thieves, knaves, and robbers,"
was the way one of them summed up the situation — he
was Moses Harvey of Montague in Hampshire County
— "and if the people do not bestir themselves they are
undone."

It was only then that the people bestirred themselves,
and even then they did nothing more revolutionary than
to take stock by calling county conventions. The movement arose as "a black cloud in the east," as an orator
later put it, in Bristol's Taunton on July 18; it spread
to Worcester's Leicester on August 15, and by late August to Hatfield in Hampshire, Concord in Middlesex,
and Lenox in Berkshire.

2.

As of 1786 Massachusetts had been governing itself
for six years under a constitution of its own designing.
One of the last states to take this step (during the early
part of the Revolution it had made shift with an adaptation of the last royal charter), it had by waiting to study
the expedients adopted by other states, achieved one of
the best.

The instrument, expertly tailored by John Adams, with some help from his cousin Sam, had eschewed the radicalism of constitutions more precipitately adopted. There was no nonsense about it as in the Pennsylvania constitution, which provided for a unicameral legislature; Massachusetts had a proper Senate to act as a brake on the more questionable impulses of the House. There was no taint of the Levelist notion that a man without property may be entrusted with the responsibility of voting away the property of others; unlike such states as Pennsylvania and New Hampshire, the Massachusetts constitution not only limited the vote to property-holders, but had upped the qualification from what it had been under the last royal charter. Office-holders were also required to have property in an ascending scale, according to their importance, until only men of near munificence could serve in the Senate.

Add to these provisions the religious oath required of officers, as was proper in what had once been a theocracy, and you had a perfect constitution. Though human imperfections had to be recognized by allowing for amendments, this was not to be done until the constitution had a full opportunity to prove its worth. For fifteen years it was to be held inviolate though the heavens fell in the meantime, as in fact they did.

The heavens fell in 1786, and they fell partly because the public at large was by no means unanimously agreed on the perfection of the new constitution. To be sure, only a handful of those intellectuals who had taken the Declaration rather literally objected to the restriction on voting. One such was the old revolutionary Joseph Hawley of Northampton, who had had much to say about what he called "the poor polls," who were taxed without representation; others were two officers in Boston's own Suffolk County, who resigned their commissions in the militia, saying: "We decline acting under such a form of government . . . that appears repugnant to our principles of freedom."

Simpler men made no difficulties largely because it had always been so and they were used to it; of Puritan stock, they had not yet renounced the old Puritan equation of righteousness with prosperity, the latter being the visible sign of God's grace. Moreover, in the phase of government that most intimately concerned them, they hardly felt the deprivation. Town meeting, when concerned with local matters, seldom counted the contents of a man's pocket before it counted his vote. Their objection was less to the restriction itself than to its effects. It gave those eastern counties where most of the wealth was concentrated a stranglehold over the lower House, and resulted in the election of a Senate so obstructive to the popular will that to the western farmer it was as if he were still ruled by the British Lords of the Admiralty. By 1786 the Senate had become as unpopular as the Lords had ever been, and Boston, once so radical, now the stronghold of conservatism, was subtly replacing Britain as the Enemy.

Once, hardly a decade earlier, western farmers had been the conservatives. They had required considerable rousing, as no one knew better than Boston's Sam Adams, before they could be induced to follow Boston down the road to revolution. But once they had been won to revolutionary methods, they had acquired a taste for them. The county convention, evolved when royal officials were trying to curb local government, had taken as deep root in their folkways as town meeting itself, and in western Massachusetts persisted long after its inventor, Sam Adams, had declared it superfluous. Six years of constitutional government had not sufficed to wean the farmers from revolutionary practice. In any time of discontent, county convention was called, and now in the summer of 1786, when Legislature adjourned without taking action on the manifold grievances of what were beginning to call themselves the People, conventions were summoned in five counties, and those very towns which had failed in their duty of sending delegates to General Court were most fully and aggressively represented.

To their irritated political superiors it looked as if the people preferred to govern themselves not by the law of the land but by this discarded revolutionary body which had no means of implementing its demands — no legal means — and no legal standing beyond the constitutional guarantee of the right of peaceable assembly.

To the country towns, however, the preference for county convention was innocent and logical. The latter met close at hand, seldom sat for more than three days, and a town which could not afford to send a man to Boston to wait six weeks or more on the Governor's pleasure could easily manage to pay not only his expenses to county convention but a modest wage besides. Some towns, in times when everyone's property was dwindling, actually had no citizen possessed of the property qualification for election to General Court. County convention, blessedly above and beyond the sacred constitution, was hampered by no such niggling restrictions.

Delegates to the conventions were elected with as much attention to protocol as delegates to General Court. Special town meeting was called for the purpose. Local windbags were bypassed for those men who could think on their feet and stick to a point without being carried away by the nasal Yankee music of their own voices. That there should be no doubt as to what the point was, town meeting instructed them.

From the Berkshires at the border of York State to
little Rehoboth at the edge of Rhode Island, the delegates
readied themselves for their duties, studying their instructions, ransacking their Bibles and sometimes a dog-
eared Plutarch for text and precedent. Their wives gave
their Sunday best a going-over with needle, brush, and
sadiron and, when the day came, helped them into it. Most
wore homespun, woven and cut to a rough fit by their
wives; on them it had the shaggy suitability of the bark
of an old butternut. Hampshire men usually wore check-
ered shirts, for peddlers from Connecticut drove a thriv-
ing trade in indigo through the Connecticut Valley, and
one could tell a man from these parts by his shirt. Those
who had been thumbing their Plutarchs still had a frayed
broadcloth handed down from a grandfather. Veterans
got into their threadbare Continental uniform; tradition-
ally these were buff and blue; in point of fact, since the
Service of Supply had never been the strong point of the
Continental Army, they might be almost any color. They
added dash to their outfits by buckling on their side arms.

They stuffed their saddlebags with bread and cheese
and even fodder for the horse, for those who, lacking
friends in convention town, had to put up at the inn, carried what supplies they could so that there would be no
charge beyond drink and board for the man and stable for
the horse.

Thus garbed, accoutered, and supplied, the delegate
got on his horse, "goose rumped and cat hammed," with
a long switch tail and a mane falling to his knees. The
master, long-legged and lank, rode his beast with a long
stirrup, and his horse set off with an "unaccountable wrig-
gling gait." So mounted, remarked a British observer —
Americans seldom looked at each other or made note of

what they saw if they did — the delegate looked like the Knight of the Woeful Countenance.

In present circumstances there was some justice in the simile.

3.

Some conventions opened in a tavern, some in the local meetinghouse; in either place the first thought was of God. The delegates bowed their heads while a Reverend "addressed the throne of grace." Then they organized themselves by electing chairman and secretary, and disposed of a troublesome point that their enemies were bound to raise against them; they made themselves constitutional by voting themselves so. Next they reassured the timid by taking a resolution against violence, and in spite of what so quickly followed, the resolution was probably more sincere than not.

Then the delegates made themselves heard.

"I've labored hard all my days and fared hard." It was "Old Plough Jogger" speaking; the newspaper correspondent who marked his words did not grant him the dignity of his name. It was a concession that a newspaperman should attend to him at all, for gatherings of bucolic characters in upcountry Massachusetts seemed of far less interest to the journals than news from London or Moscow. The fashion was to ignore the conventions except as an opportunity for the exercise of wit; another correspondent claimed that the grievances of country folk ran to items like growing hard of hearing or a wife's persistence in having a baby a year.

Such were grievances true enough, and Old Plough Jogger may have shared them. But he had come to convention not to contest acts of God but those inequities which it was within Legislature's province to rectify. Having got the floor, he was speaking his mind slowly, earnestly, and with no more embarrassment than he spoke it in his own town meeting.

"I have been greatly abused," he went on, "have been obliged to do more than my part in the war; been loaded with class rates, town rates, province rates, Continental rates and all rates . . . been pulled and hauled by sheriffs, constables and collectors, and had my cattle sold for less than they were worth."

There was a buzz of comment at this remark. Most of the men here, as the correspondent had ascertained, were "deep in debt," several years behind in their taxes, "and it would fare hard with them if the law took its course." Many had already "fared hard," had been haled to the hated Court of Common Pleas for nonpayment of debt, had judgment found against them with the court costs added to the original sum; had watched helplessly while the constable sold their property at a "vendue," and since nothing in hard times fetched more than a fraction of its worth, had the humiliation of losing their oxen without the satisfaction of settling the debt.

Such events had recently evoked an ugly spirit of resistance. In Worcester and Berkshire counties men had banded together to repossess from the constable the livestock confiscated from a good neighbor. It was an object of the convention to find means of making such incidents unnecessary. By now nearly everyone was indebted to everyone else: yeoman to laborer, laborer to merchant, son to father, uncle to cousin. Everyone knew good men whom creditors had forced into debtors' prison. Everyone was faced with the specter of losing not only his livestock but the land itself, and with his land his standing as a freeman. Serfdom lay ahead of them if matters took their

present course, for how else does a man become a serf but in this way? The convention had come together to find the means of staying this course.

Old Plough Jogger still had the floor.

"I have been obliged to pay and nobody will pay me. I have lost a great deal by this man and that man and t'other man, and the great men are going to get all we have, and I think it is time for us to rise and put a stop to it, and have no more courts, nor sheriffs, nor collectors, nor lawyers, and I know that we are the biggest party, let them say what they will."

The chairman brought his gavel down sharply on the applause. Old Plough Jogger had exceeded his rights. The convention was here to put a stop to these inequities, but not by rising up. A constitutional body it had voted itself, and under the constitution it would proceed. Its function was that of a sounding-board, a kind of lobby organized at the grass roots to bring pressure to bear on Legislature. Its business was to assemble the legitimate grievances of the likes of Old Plough Jogger and present them in a petition of such force that Legislature could not again ignore them.

To this business the convention applied itself.

4.

It was a complicated, difficult business. The convention men were by no means politically illiterate. They had been seasoned not only by working out the details of town government in town meeting, always the bedrock of Massachusetts government, but by dealing with the larger issues in such revolutionary bodies as the committees of correspondence and of safety, and a long series of county conventions.

With this measure of political sophistication, however,

went several limitations. On many issues they were ill informed. The fact that the seat of state government was
in Boston — this was large among their grievances —
gave them an imperfect grasp on its details. Its remoteness
deprived them of the privilege enjoyed by Boston of
watching General Court in action. Few of them ever saw
a newspaper. There had been sporadic publications in
Springfield and Pittsfield; in Northampton a young Connecticut Yankee named William Butler was even now
carting in his newsprint in preparation for publishing the
Hampshire Gazette; Worcester had Isaiah Thomas's excellent *Massachusetts Spy.* But most papers were published in Boston and circulated little outside. Farmers
were dependent on hearsay for information. Many of
them genuinely believed that the present intolerable taxes
had one simple purpose: to enable state officials to live
in luxury.

Inadequately informed about their own Legislature,
their perception was dim indeed about that remoter entity, Continental Congress, now sitting in a "foreign government," in New York. Ever since the renunciation of
the more comprehensible concept of personal loyalty to a
king, national government had been for them in a state
of nebular hypothesis. In this they were not alone; their
apparent intellectual superiors in Boston, when they were
honest, acknowledged a sense of moving in worlds not
realized. In spite of the structure of orderly government
raised by state constitutions and the Articles of Confederation, the "state of nature" induced by the destructive
agencies of the Revolution still prevailed in the hearts and
minds of many men of good will.

In particular they could not grasp why the triumphant
conclusion of the Revolution should, after one brief, illusory period of prosperity, have plunged them into a

grave economic crisis. True, the war had been long and costly, but there had been long and costly wars before without this result. The men of the conventions of 1786 forbore drawing conclusions which some of them had not hesitated to draw in 1782 when there had been an analogous if briefer crisis: that they had been better off under the last royal governors than they were now under governors of their own election. Nor did they call attention to the fact that one difference was that in the old wars against the French and Indians, the mother country had borne much of the expense. They could hardly expect that benevolence from what was no longer the mother country as a result of a war whose purpose had been independence. Such as it was, independence was now an accomplished fact; they had no quarrel with it. Their trouble was that under present circumstances independence didn't seem applicable to them.

The conventions drew up statements in something of the manner of the great Declaration. They highly resolved; they set forth their grievances.

The Hampshire convention resolved that the constitution should be revised at once without any talk of waiting fifteen years, that General Court relieve a penniless people by establishing a bank of paper money, that it reassemble at once to accomplish these ends and take action on grievances.

The latter made a long list. At the head was the existence of those two instruments of oppression, the Senate and the Court of Common Pleas. Then there was the rapacity of the legal profession and the exorbitance of the court fee table; the meeting of General Court in Boston, the high salaries of government officials, and nearly the entire structure of the heavy taxes of 1785.

The Bristol County resolutions deplored "the calami-

tous circumstances" of debtors forced to sell their property at a quarter of its real value, announced "a terrible
catastrophe" if grievances were not remedied, and cried
out against pronouncements that industry alone would
solve their problems. They were industrious, they said,
but the products of their industry spoiled because no one
had money to buy.

One Bristol County man, George Brock, reinforced
this statement by an "Address to the Yeomanry of Massachusetts," published in Boston's *Independent Chronicle*
over the signature of "Attleborough," his town. The
yeomanry, he said, had won liberty only to be faced at
home with new enemies in the courts, "the placemen, the
pensioners, and above all that aristocratical people too
generally prevalent among the wealthy men of the state."
It was these who stigmatized as traitors any who dared
inquire into their mismanagement, and who sneered at
simple men for living in "luxury."

"The extreme distress the people have suffered [for
want of] food of the most homely kind gives the lie
direct" to such charges, said Attleborough, "and unless
their intended lordships are resolved that we should follow the example of the oppressed Irish and live wholly
on potatoes and skimmed milk, I know not what method
of support they have charted out for us."

The business of the conventions concluded, the delegates dispersed to report to their town meetings. The
clerks labored to make fair copies of the resolutions, not
only for presentation to General Court, but for the information of other conventions. There was nothing to do now
but wait on General Court to act.

That was the theory. The pressure of need and of
precedent impelled a rather different practice. In very
recent history the conventions had been only one stage of

revolutionary development; they had been immediately followed by another stage equally hallowed by the name of patriotism. It was logical, honorable, and eminently good sense that history follow this course again.

Without waiting on General Court to come back in session to work on grievances as requested, the People took matters into their own hands.

CHAPTER II

Day at Court

Talk about Northampton court had been going on for a long time. All well and proper to petition, the farmers were telling each other, but General Court couldn't act on the petitions until it met, and unfortunately the Court of Common Pleas was meeting first. For those on whom it passed judgment the relief anticipated from General Court would come too late. Judgment would be passed, execution ordered, oxen seized, even fields lost just as they were ripe for harvest.

The talk had gone on in the taverns, in kitchens with the young ones listening all ears, among knots of men lingering by the horseblocks after Sabbath meeting. Out of the talk had matured a plan, and the night before court it became a certainty.

"You with us at the doin's in town tomorrow?"

"Can't. I've no one to look after my creatures."

"My boy Jonas'll be over. You come with us."

Across the haymows, the stone walls, up the mountain acres spiced with the scent of sweet fern, into the barns, the word was called that August evening. There were scores of people like Abraham Smith — for such was the father of Jonas — going about their own corner of

Hampshire County, passing the word along. It might have been the day before Lexington.

On August 29 in the hour before sunup it was more like Lexington than ever. The womenfolk and children watched their men swing their muskets to their shoulders and set out, boys like Jonas resentfully, for it was hard, when there were doings, to stay home, and mind other folks' cattle. The eyes of some women were anxious. It was too much like Lexington; it had been a long time of trouble after, and the men not settled from it yet.

But other women set their lips. "It's about time," they said.

The men disappeared into the mists lying in the hollows. The women pulled their ragged shawls about them against the early-morning chill and padded about on bare feet to begin the chores. To hear the Boston papers tell it, one would suppose that farm women went to the milkstool as fancily dressed as Marie Antoinette at the Petit Trianon; that was because some measure of the general indebtedness was owed the merchants, who had eagerly pressed credit on the farmers in the brave days at the close of the Revolution when the ports were reopened and "foreign superfluities" became available again. To please their womenfolk, farmers had run up bills for stuffs like calicoes and tammies, even sometimes a silk kerchief or a brass kettle, and these bills were still largely unpaid.

Even in the best of times, however, no one wasted good clothes on chores. What one had of best was saved for the social occasions when neighbors were invited in for a "sit down," or for Sabbath meeting. In warm weather most folks set out barefoot for meeting, stopping within sight of the meetinghouse to pull on shoes too good for common wear.

Now the woman whistled up the dog, who streaked it

up to the pasture and began his own chore, rushing and snapping at the heels of the herd. The cows were runts; the fine points of breeding — as of scientific husbandry generally — were little understood hereabouts, though there was mention of such things in some almanacs, along with reminders to farmers that larger, better-bred cows were an economy; fewer of them would provide the family supply of milk and cheese, and since taxes were rated at so much a head, this was a legitimate way of cutting them.

Underbred or not, the fawn-like little cattle had spirit. At the snapping of the dog they wheeled and came galloping down the hill in fine fettle. The farm wife kneaded and worked their udders and the milk squirted into the wooden pails. At the sound the cat strolled down from the haymow, and the hogs, hopefully squealing and grunting, trotted in from the wood lot. They were a keen-witted, intrepid lot, these pigs, descendants of the wild boars of old England. They were capable of thrusting an inquiring snout into Sabbath meeting, of giving battle to a wildcat, and they relished nothing more than a meal of rattlesnake.

From the yard outside the gaunt, unpainted little farmhouse came the clank of bucket in well as the lad came out to fetch the water. In the kitchen the little girls rattled the pewter dishes from cupboard to table and peered into the black pot steaming over the fireplace. The children ran to flaxen hair in these parts, and their faces even under the sunburn were fair, for this was the "not Angles but angels" type. But when they opened their mouths, the teeth of some already showed black. The teeth of Americans were the horror of foreign visitors, who spun philosophies to explain why so well-set-up a people, as a race lean and tall — for the runtishness of the beasts did not infect their masters — should have such bad teeth.

Farm folk dispensed with the philosophy. If their teeth

were bad, it was God's providence; they endured the decay, and when it ached, they pulled.

The kitchen, in which the woman now slapped down her buckets, was the living-room of the house. Few homes hereabouts had more than two rooms, except for the gentry, and the carefully guarded New England parlor, with its carpets, its curtains, its store furniture, had yet to be invented. Carpets there were none, and the rugs were a rare bearskin or, more commonly, the pelt of the old farm dog, serviceable even in death, his shagginess giving comfort to shrinking feet on a bitter morning.

"Oh Jum," the farm wife would address an aging dog, "I hope when you die it'll be winter, when your fur is good."

The walls were wattled with clay and in some houses whitewashed. Herbs and ears of corn hung drying from the low rafters, and blended their scent with the good woody smell of the place. Floors laid with sawed boards, as against split logs, were cleanly covered with sand from the town sand lot. The furniture was spare and strictly functional: a table, a fireside settle, chairs and stools, knocked together by the husbandman and his sons, though some had chairs rush-bottomed by a neighbor in return for the "old white-faced cow" or a length of homespun.

The woman bent over the black pot at the fire to see if the hasty pudding — a dish of corn that belied its name, for it took hours to boil — was ready. A girl broke the bread in hunks and went to the crock that held what was left of the maple syrup from last spring's boiling in the sugarbush. Store-bought molasses was a more genteel sweetening, but too much was owed at the store already, and there were some who actually preferred the taste of maple. Another brought in from the storehouse, cut into the bank, some of the shad taken from the Connecticut in

the spring running and salted down against the time when
the last side of pork had gone and fall slaughter was still
some weeks off. It used to be that Connecticut Valley folk
were sensitive to the charge that they ate shad — they
caught it only for sport, they liked to say — for it was a
disgrace not to have pork in abundant supply. Just now
few were squeamish about shad.

"For what we are about to receive," muttered the
woman, having ladled the hasty pudding into a basin and
set it on the table, where the children could reach it with
their porringers. The sun was up now and blazed through
the open door.

"Think Pa's got to town yet?" asked the older girl.

It was what the mother had been wondering; but she
wasn't going to talk about it. "Eat what's before you and
get to your churning," she said. "I have to look at the
fields."

For she was one of the women who got favorable mention in the taverns. "I married me a wife, and a fine young
working woman she was," her husband bragged.

She still was. Up in the field she studied the stand of
grass, the looks of the sky west over Mount Tom, and
went to the barn to get what her man spelled in his nota-
tions in his almanac as the "sithe." There was a pleasant
community of labor between men and women on the
farms. There were veterans of the Continental line who
turned their hands to weaving; there were women who
liked sometimes a day in the fields, finding still in their
arms the strength and endurance that had got them
through the Revolution.

2.

Down in the valley the people of Northampton had
already been drawn out of doors by the stir in the streets.

They came out not to participate but to look on, and someone had already gone to call Sheriff Elisha Porter. Respectable people lived here; they did not hold with irregular goings-on, and had scorned to send a delegate to the Hatfield convention. If there had been rioting here four years ago when Samuel Ely had stirred up the county, it was no fault of theirs. Grievances then as now centered around court, and it was the turn of Northampton, half-shire town of Hampshire, the Texas of Massachusetts counties, to have court today. It would gladly have surrendered its turn to Springfield, the other shire town. Farmers from the upper county, loud in their complaints at having to come so far to answer a court summons, were coming in today unsummoned.

Northampton was a pretty town, its vistas looking into the broad river and the sharp little peaks of Mount Holyoke and Mount Tom, and it was in normal times prosperous. Its lands on the loamy intervals of the Connecticut were the fattest and blackest and best in the county. Such landowners, who had the further advantage of being able to float their produce downstream to Hartford, a more accessible commercial capital than Boston, were the "river gods." Of the three hundred houses, each set in its garden and orchard on the ten grassy streets that crawled out crabwise from the center of town, they had the largest. Some had high-ceiled rooms that were not wattled or whitewashed, but plastered and papered; they had the carpets, the brocaded draperies, the polished furniture, and the silver plate from England, all the "foreign superfluities" that farmers were accused of having and seldom saw.

All this was as it should be; they had prospered because God had prospered them.

Of all the river gods of Northampton there was only

one who might have watched the invasion with sympathetic comprehension. Joseph Hawley, who had once startled Northampton town meeting with his advocacy of universal suffrage, who had in a similar disturbance in 1782 prevailed upon Boston to deal with the malcontents not by force but by giving them a patient hearing, should have been out to meet the people from upcountry. But Hawley had succumbed to an ancestral melancholia. "He is dead while he yet liveth," they said of him in Northampton. Today he sat withdrawn in his chamber, his eyes fixed on blankness, his mind gone as dead as the coal in the pipe on which he insatiably sucked. As more people went by on their way to the courthouse and their voices rose, Hawley's wife, Mercy, came in and gently drew the curtains.

When the farmers straggled into town in pairs, in squads, in companies, they were taken in hand and organized into something like military order by veterans of the Continental Army. Conspicuous among the veterans was Hawley's old acquaintance Captain Luke Day of West Springfield.

They had met in April 1782, on the occasion when the agitator Samuel Ely had led a miscellaneous mob to the woodpile with the intent of finding clubs to use against the judges of Northampton court and "knock their gray wigs off." Luke Day had been one of a group of veterans who had defended court and protected the judges from this indignity.

Afterwards Hawley had talked with these veterans and had learned that they no less than the mob were obsessed with a burning sense of grievance. They had received little pay in the service, and on discharge had got their arrears in the form of state certificates which were redeemable with interest, but only in the future, and in the meantime

were not negotiable at all. The only way the veterans
could get cash to meet their obligations had been to sell
the certificates to sharpers, who, with large gestures of
self-sacrifice, snapped them up at a fraction of face value.

"You cannot hear them speak of the matter but in rage
and flame," Hawley had then reported of the likes of
Luke Day. "They are a fierce lot of men. . . . It signi-
fied nothing to tell these folks that their interest will be
made on principle when the collector is at the door demanding hard cash. They . . . burst out in rage and
became desperate. . . . You may rely upon it that they
are on the point of turning to the mob, and if they are not
relieved . . . they will become outrageous, and the numbers who will side with them will be irresistible. Your
sheriffs will be like stubble before devouring fire. . . ."

Four years later the prophecy had come true. Luke Day
and his kind had turned to the mob and become "outrageous"; the numbers that sided with them were irresistible, and the Hampshire sheriff, Elisha Porter, though a
plain man not given to metaphor, would agree that he was
like stubble before a devouring fire.

In 1782 Luke Day, in spite of his private sentiments,
had loyally stayed the course of law and order, had defended court in April and again in June. But the succeed-
ing years of deprivation had convinced him that his loyalty
had been misplaced. The pittance he had received for his
certificates had not sufficed to meet his obligations. In
1785 he had been put in debtors' prison. For two stifling
summer months Day, a proud man, had endured the stinking confinement of Northampton jail in the society of
murderers, counterfeiters, and common thieves.

It had not been for this that he had stayed with the
Revolution full term, and recently, in the pride of his
record, had put in his application to what ungrateful

civilians called the "aristocratical" order of the Cincinnati. On August 29 he had broken jail and his bond and gone home to West Springfield.

Since then he had been much in the taverns among those who brooded over the blasting of the bright hopes of the Revolution by present inequities. By 1786 veterans had a new grievance, beyond the common misery of debts and taxes; at long last Massachusetts was preparing to redeem with interest the old securities, now almost wholly in the hands of the speculators. Far from receiving their due, the veterans were to be taxed to assure the sharpers their profit.

The taverns were by no means necessarily disreputable places; a minister might stop there for a dram. Whether in the tavern or elsewhere, Luke Day saw much of his pastor, the Reverend Joseph Lathrop, and expounded to him a text which seemed to him divinely inspired to describe the grievous condition of Massachusetts.

"Then I returned and saw all the oppressions that are done under the sun: and behold, the tears of such as were oppressed, and they had no comforter; and on the side of their oppressors there was power, but they had no comforter. Wherefore I praised the dead which are already dead more than the living which are yet alive."

But the pastor refused to agree to the meaning that Captain Day read into the verses from Ecclesiastes. It was for man, said the pastor, to endure patiently all the manifestations of God's inscrutable will, debtors' prison included. Day had high respect for his pastor's opinion and would consult it often, but he did not hold himself bound by it.

He had slept little on the eve of Northampton court. All evening he had been riding about West Springfield, readying his friends, and soon after midnight he had them

on the march on the long road to Northampton. His party
was the first to arrive. To the thrilling strain of its fife-
and-drum corps the last sleepers awoke, and looking out,
saw ranks stepping down the square to the courthouse as
smartly as if Steuben in person were in command.

As it happened, it was the anniversary of the day on
which Luke Day had escaped from debtors' prison. He
was here to settle in his own way his accounts with court.

3.

In 1782 Joseph Hawley had forecast not only the present conduct of Luke Day's kind, but with equal accuracy
the effect on local authority. "Were they the common
enemy, we could bear it," he had written, "but they are
our equals, our acquaintances, our brethren . . . impossible for us to defend ourselves against our brethren."

At least Sheriff Elisha Porter, a humane man, and inclined to lenience when lenience was practicable, found it
impossible. Summoned on the approach of Day, his first
thought indeed was to call out the militia to take the situation in hand. But then he saw what gave him to pause;
much of the militia was already present, and it was en-
thusiastically taking orders from Day.

While Porter reflected on the complexities of the situation, others came in, stragglers and small parties from
everywhere, a company from Amherst under Lieutenant
Billings, another company, as well set up as Day's, with its
own fife and drum, representing the combined forces of
Pelham in the hills and Greenwich in the hollow, led by
a Captain Hinds. Porter was taking note of provenance
and names, but Billingses were as thick in Amherst and
Hindses in Greenwich as Days were in Springfield, and
he wasn't always sure which one was which.

By midday he had given up all thought of opposing the

invaders; their ranks had swelled to at least five hundred
and they were still coming. The weight of their numbers
and a certain determination in their temper resolved him,
as he explained to Boston, "not by any means to oppose or
irritate them, but to treat them with civility."

In the meantime the judges had put on the black silk
robes which they wore in summer and waited for Porter
to lead them in solemn procession to the courthouse. Porter got out his long wand, emblem of authority, and
gravely performed this duty.

But at the courthouse there was a more potent emblem
of authority, the bayonets of the men Luke Day had stationed there. Day stood with them, holding a petition
drafted during the morning. It asserted the People's constitutional right to protest unconstitutional acts of the
recent Legislature and "entreated" the judges to adjourn
until the "minds of the people can be obtained and the
resolves of the convention of this county can have an opportunity of having their grievances redressed by General
Court."

The judges, retiring to Samuel Clark's tavern, exam-
ined this petition, then cast it aside and waited. The
demonstration had caught them by surprise and they had
no plan of action. Yet it was unthinkable that the court
actually be stopped. Not even Ely's far more rowdy mob
in 1782 had succeeded to that extent. The good citizens of
Northampton were as outraged as they, and, given time,
would restore order.

The good citizens of Northampton, however, mindful
of the safety of their stores, their barns, and of the very
glass in their windows, had no appetite for action that
might provoke retaliation, and time worked on the side
of the invaders. By late afternoon their numbers were

estimated at close to fifteen hundred. At nightfall the judges gave in; they adjourned "without day."

"They aimin' to hold court at night?" demanded someone, and lest the judges have such designs, some men held the courthouse until well after midnight.

But the dispersal was orderly. The farmers went back to their farms, hung up their muskets, and turned to belated chores, for in spite of the dependability of most womenfolk, a few found forgotten cows "bellerin'" to be milked. Northampton was left in peace, but not without a sense of outrage.

"Prison full of criminals and none can be punished," a Southampton man, Jonathan Judd, wrote in the little notebook he kept for observations on haying and weather, natural and political. "Monarchy is better than the tyranny of the mob."

CHAPTER III

"*Liberty Is Still the Object*"

Had the Northampton incident happened in isolation, it might have been passed over, and the ugly name of rebellion never applied. But this could not be. Throughout Massachusetts the fall sessions of the Court of Common Pleas were about to sit, and in all those counties which had held conventions, those who called themselves the People were determined to prevent them.

The next court was scheduled for Tuesday, September 5, in Worcester County, Hampshire's next neighbor to the east. That it would be opposed had been suspected for a long time. Even before the convention a circular letter had gone through the county calling on the people to rise up against court. Since then there had been a second letter, published in the *Spy,* urging that the people do nothing so rash; but this letter represented only one man's opinion and exerted no great influence. Enemies of the court noted that the date was within one day of the anniversary of the closing of the same court by patriots in the early stages of the Revolution. They were patriots still, and in that spirit they would act.

Shire town of Worcester County was Worcester town. Its situation was less picturesque than Northampton's, for it had no such river as the Connecticut, and though its ways lay at the foot of craggy little hills, the only peak in the county, Mount Wachusett, lay well to the north, beyond the uplands of Petersham and Hubbardston. The town itself, however, with its well-built houses, its neatly fenced, well-tended grounds and gardens, gave an equal impression of orderly living and prosperity. It was much spoken of as a more proper state capital than Boston.

It was also a town of culture in that it had the gifted publisher Isaiah Thomas, and his manifold printing-presses. His *Massachusetts Spy* had as much influence as any paper in Boston. Lately the *Spy* had suspended publication. Editor Thomas, having taken note of the times by signifying his willingness to accept payment for subscriptions in cordwood and farm produce, had implemented his vehement protest against taxes by converting the *Spy* into the *Worcester Magazine*. It was an irreproachable measure of tax-evasion; papers were subject to the new Stamp Act; magazines were not.

Newspaper or magazine, Thomas's publications continued to combine dazzling displays of erudition with the saltiest of journalism. One week, readers were treated to a criticism of Pope's *Iliad*, illustrated by printing in parallel columns a segment of Pope's translation and of Homer's text in the original Greek. In the next they got full treatment of a rape in Vermont down to its most cloacal details. Whenever or wherever there was a suicide, Thomas got the story, reported the state of the corpse with gusto, and added editorial comment on the cowardice of men who chose to leave "their stinking carcasses hanging." Many suicides were Negroes, and he remarked with concern that some homesick whites were adopting the Negro superstition that the soul of a suicide returned to its native land.

Nor did Thomas ever miss the more legal kind of hanging. These, being public and advertised in advance, had already been observed by readers able to get to town for the solemn and edifying spectacle. But the casual visitor could not do what Thomas invariably did — get to the cell of the condemned on the eve of the execution and induce a true confession complete with warnings to the young. Such a scoop was too valuable to be included in the price of subscription; it was made available in bound copies sold separately and advertised in the *Spy*.

Isaiah Thomas's sensitive nose for news had smelled out the signs of trouble almost before anybody; as early as July he had picked up a rumor that court was to be attacked.

Thanks to the influence on Worcester town meeting of such a citizen, Worcester town had sent no delegate to the Worcester County convention. Worcester was in fact currently torn by quite irrelevant troubles, the question of a successor to the old minister, who had died early in the spring. The church had split on the question, and Thomas and the apothecary Abraham Lincoln led a powerful minority that demanded the right to found a parish of their own. So far they had been unsuccessful, but in the months to come, while rival armies marched and countermarched through Worcester, this quarrel would remain the principal subject of Worcester town meeting.

But when the farmers came to town Worcester forgot its parish quarrel and went out on the streets to watch the show.

2.

It was a good show. And its hero was, rather unexpectedly, Chief Justice Artemas Ward.

Judge Ward had also been at Northampton, and had maintained his dignity there in spite of the difficulties. His failure to oppose the insurgents more vigorously had been due to the effect of surprise, to the diffidence of the sheriff, and to the fact that state authorities had issued no directive to cover such a situation. Today in Worcester there was no surprise. Ward's home was in near-by Shrewsbury; his fellow townsmen were loud in their complaint against government in general and judges in particular, and he knew what to expect. Sheriff William Greenleaf would do what he was told, and, best of all, there was now a government directive.

On September 2 Governor Bowdoin had issued a proclamation. It denounced the Northampton incident as a highhanded attempt "to subvert all law and government and introduce riot, anarchy and confusion, which would probably terminate in absolute despotism, consequently destroying the fairest prospects of political happiness that any people was ever favored with." He called on the people to assist their officers in suppressing "such treasonable proceedings."

The powers of the sheriff in such an emergency had been clarified for the Governor by Judge Theophilus Parsons. The statement had not been published, but Ward was cognizant of and fortified by its contents. The sheriff should use only persuasion to disperse a mob which waited quietly, but he was to collect the militia, and if the mob did not respond to persuasion, to order the militia to fire; and the militia must follow orders.

Unpleasant to fire, but today Judge Ward remembered that he had also been a general. He had once stood in George Washington's shoes, or, rather, Washington had stepped into his, for it was from him that Washington had received command of the Massachusetts troops after his appointment by Continental Congress. Ward had taken his disappointment gracefully, and had presently bowed out, being indeed too old and infirm for active service.

But today, looking out from the house where he and his colleagues had assembled, seeing in the courthouse square two hundred men, at least half of them armed, Judge Ward became the soldier again. He didn't look it; his silken robes billowed about an aging figure of enormous, unmilitary girth. But he had the spirit that wins battles, and in that spirit he gave his orders.

The town crier and Sheriff Greenleaf led the way, and the judges followed in grave procession, quite as if this were a usual day in court with no one to bar the way.

The way was barred. A sentinel leveled his gun at them, and in the gun a bayonet was fixed.

"What's your business here?" snapped Ward, and the sentinel, who had been one of his own subalterns in a happier day, fell back in confusion and, instead of stopping the judicial progress, presented arms to his general.

The judges went on. Before the courthouse stood a file of men with fixed bayonets, and before them a graying veteran with drawn sword. The town crier turned to the chief justice inquiringly.

"Go cry the court," said Ward.

His voice still conveyed command. The file on the steps actually parted to let the crier through, and no one lifted a hand to stop him when he threw open the door. But the courtroom was occupied; a squad of infantry leveled their muskets on the judges from just inside the door.

The ranks closed again when Ward made to follow.

"Who is your leader, and what are you doing here?" he demanded. And when there was no answer: "I say, who is your leader?"

It was a question no one was prepared to answer. Leaders there obviously were; as at Northampton, each town's company had its own. The men from Barre were taking orders from Moses Smith, presently to be reported as an insolent fellow; Princeton had followed the lead of the Gale brothers, Henry and Abraham; and the gray veteran who barred the way to the courthouse with his sword, Adam Wheeler, had charge of the men from Hubbardston. Nevertheless, a leader in any official sense there was none. Apparently no one had thought of it, and there was that in Judge Ward's manner that inspired a certain reluctance to claim the distinction. But he was insisting.

"I'm not the leader," said Wheeler, "but I can tell you what we're here for. We've come to relieve the distresses of the people. There will be no court until they have redress of their grievances."

Ward glanced at the sheriff, on whom now devolved the duty of dispersing the "mob" by persuasion. But persuasion was not one of the gifts of Sheriff Greenleaf; he was, moreover, unpopular among the people, who would eventually succeed in ousting him from office. The judge, on the other hand, had had some success as a persuader. In 1782 he had been sent into Hampshire County in response to Hawley's plea, as one of a committee assigned by General Court to reason with the aggrieved followers of Ely. The mission had been remarkably successful — though somehow Sam Adams had got most of the credit. Ward now proposed to repeat the experiment.

Captain Moses Smith roughly pushed forward to prevent him. "Put it in writing!" said Smith, and at his command the bayonets converged on the judge.

"I'm not afraid of your bayonets!" snapped Ward. "You've been deceiving these people. Give me a position where they can hear me and I'll prove it to them."

"They haven't come to listen to your long speeches," retorted Smith, and ordered the drums to beat and the guard to charge. The bayonets pressed in on Ward, pierc-

ing his silken robes. But the man didn't budge. All that
the charge accomplished was exposure of the not unamia-
ble weakness of the chargers. It wasn't in them to run him
through; they were decent people, and in spite of themselves they were won to admiration for the bulky, elderly
figure which, unarmed, held its own against cold steel.

For nearly two hours Judge Ward addressed the crowd
in the square, exposing the "fallacy" of the "supposed
grievances," pointing out that only civil war and anarchy
could result from the method of redress chosen, and ex-
pounding the meaning of treason.

What was remarkable was that for those two hours the
men in the square gave him their attention. Sabbath meeting had accustomed them to long listening, had even given
them a taste for it. They interrupted him sometimes, but
they heard him out. Some flinched from his reference to
the gallows as the penalty for treason, and one insurgent
listened so carefully that he repented and when he got
home wrote a letter saying so and sent it to Isaiah
Thomas, who printed it.

The exhortation was stopped at last, not by subversive
action, but by rain. Judge Ward's robes were getting wet.
"May the sun never shine on rebellion in Massachusetts!" he concluded dramatically, and retired to the
United States Arms. It was an invocation that might once
have got him accused of witchcraft, for it happened that
the sun was thereafter seldom to shine on the insurgents.
The weather came out solidly on the side of government.

3.

The judge's eloquence had not, however, got him into
the courthouse. In the afternoon Ward and his colleagues
were put to the now familiar expedient of opening court
in the tavern and waiting for the militia, which Sheriff

Greenleaf had been sent to muster. They waited in vain.
Some of the militia already stood in the square barring
the courthouse from its lawful occupants. The rest, being
approached, ordered, and expostulated with, reminded of
the Governor's proclamation, only murmured their regrets. Deprecatingly their officers said that their men,
though of varying sentiments, were unanimously against
interfering.

Nor did the private citizens of Worcester take any interest in forming a posse to defend court in the manner
suggested by the Governor. The sympathies of many lay
with the insurgents; others were not looking for trouble,
for though the insurgents were less numerous than they
had been in Northampton, they were well organized,
determined, and frequently reinforced. No telling how
many might come if serious opposition were made them.
Most of Worcester looked on in a "go-it-bear, go-it-
husband" sort of mood.

If the insurgents were stubborn, so was Judge Ward.
It was not until Wednesday afternoon that he gave up
and adjourned the Court of Common Pleas "without day"
as requested, and the Court of Sessions, to the impotent
exasperation of the insurgents, to November 21.

There had been in the meantime incidents. On Tuesday
afternoon Moses Smith, sword in hand, invaded the tavern where the judges sat pensively over their mugs of
toddy, and "with great insolence" gave them half an hour
to do as ordered. The judges ignored him.

Late in the evening a more respectful committee of the
insurgents came to reason with the judges; the judges
listened to them, but refused to make promises.

Both factions spent the night in town, the judges in the
tavern, most of the insurgents in the courthouse. Next
morning the latter formed their ranks in the square, beat

their drums, and paraded around town, calling on the spectators to join them. Reinforcements had brought their numbers to four hundred.

Athol town meeting had in the meantime sent in a petition which enabled the judges to resolve the impasse without loss of face. The petition asked them to judge no civil cases except by consent of both parties; it was phrased with suitable deference and originated in a legal body whose deliberations the judges could rightfully recognize. It was in response to Athol town meeting, not to the hurly-burly in the square, that they ultimately adjourned.

Judges and insurgents departed to their respective homes, neither side content.

Judge Ward had the satisfaction of having dealt firmly with the lawbreakers. Even so, he had in the end surrendered; only to law-abiding Athol, of course, but as it happened that Athol wanted substantially what the insurgents did, the difference was rather technical.

In Shrewsbury he kept his eyes open, and when other courts were closed — for with a celerity that staggered Boston, as fast as courts could open in the disaffected counties, they were slammed shut again — he reported his observations to Governor Bowdoin.

On one occasion he had seen men from foreign parts pass through Shrewsbury on a sinister errand. "Yorkers," they called themselves, which meant New York, which was foreign enough for any proper Massachusetts man. Judge Ward began to suspect that British perfidy was behind the whole movement, and wrote to tell Governor Bowdoin so.

Adam Wheeler in Hubbardston was having afterthoughts of his own. The lack of responsible leadership exposed by Judge Ward's inquiry troubled him; so did the inadequacy of the response to the judge's eloquence.

Wheeler was not the least remarkable of what were now being called the insurgents. He was a man in his fifties, and a veteran, as it were, of two world wars; he had served against the French and Indians, and at the call of Lexington had set out in command of a company of one hundred. He stood high in the councils of his pleasant little town, and whatever he did, whatever Boston said of him, Hubbardston would never disown him.

Back at home he worked with a committee of several towns to devise a kind of grass-roots substitute for the Court of Common Pleas, to provide a board of arbitration in debtors' cases so that there would be no more vendues "to the amazing disadvantage of the debtors."

The document included a defense of recent insurgent conduct as a reply to Judge Ward. The action had not been taken, "as has injuriously been reported, to subvert all government and throw all things into a state of anarchy and confusion," but "to relieve the distresses of . . . fellow citizens until redress of grievances . . . could be obtained in the General Court. . . . We sincerely deprecate the consequences of anarchy, and we regret to transact anything contrary to the laws of the Commonwealth, but . . . we are induced by the ties of friendship and by, as we trust, the stronger laws which religion inculcates, of doing as we would be done by."

Even that statement, surely as moving as any by Judge Ward, did not wholly satisfy Wheeler. It had several signatories, among them Moses Smith. To wipe away any possible impression that he was afraid to take responsibility for his own acts, he must speak for himself.

"We have lately emerged from a bloody war in which liberty was the glorious prize aimed at," wrote Wheeler. "I earnestly stepped forth in defense of this country, and cheerfully fought to gain this prize, and liberty is still the object I have in view." His motive in stopping court had not been "to destroy public government," but was in consequence of his distress in seeing "valuable and industrious members of society dragged from their farms to prison, to the great damage not only of their families but the community at large."

To this document, ignoring the practice of the gentry, who affected classical pseudonyms whenever they undertook in the public prints to view with alarm, he signed his own honest name and sent it to the *Worcester Magazine*. And Isaiah Thomas, mindful that he had been accused of giving space only to friends of the government, printed it — just above a prescription for the cure of the bite of a mad dog.

There had been throughout much of New England a plague of rabies in the months preceding the disorders, and the elder Mathers, had they been alive, would certainly have seen God's providence in the circumstance, God's explicit commentary on the political madness already in ferment. Thomas, child of the Enlightenment, was not an editor to say much about God's providence in his columns. But by the subtle uses of make-up he got much the same effect.

CHAPTER IV

Voice of the People

The lawful source of authority in Massachusetts still emanated from within the mellowing red bricks of what the royal governors had known as the Town House. Even before the last of them had gone, however, it had become, thanks to the semantic exercises of Sam Adams, the State House. It stood at the corner of Washington and State streets; in royal times it had stood at the junction of Marlborough and King. The spot, however, was the same; the Council Chamber on the eastern end still overlooked the thicket of masts clustered about the waterfront and closer at hand the spot hallowed by the blood of those Bostonians slain by badgered British sentries in the Boston Massacre.

At two in the afternoon on Sunday, September 10, Governor Bowdoin took his place at the head of the long council table and looked into the faces of his advisors. The situation was extraordinary; public business was not often conducted on the Sabbath even in these lax times when so many of the sons of the ancient theocrats had turned to the Deist and Unitarian heresies. The body itself was extraordinary. It was not the official Governor's Council, but such of it as happened to be in town during the recess of General Court, supplemented by public-spirited citizens

43

on whom the Governor counted for wisdom. One of the latter was Sam Adams.

The Governor fated to direct Massachusetts through this crisis was an honest, plain-spoken man of sound substance and more than ordinary intellect. He was a philosopher whose correspondence even in the days of what some called the commotions, and some by the ugly name of rebellion, was concerned not only with the political turbulence of Massachusetts, but with the higher, soul-renewing concerns of the stars in their courses and the lightning his friend Franklin had plucked from the clouds. At the moment his attention was grounded on acutely temporal matters.

He owed his position to the fact that John Hancock, always the preference of Massachusetts as Governor, had retired in 1785 on the grounds of ill-health. Bowdoin could have excused himself with better reason. Hancock was gouty, and only intermittently so; Bowdoin was phthisic. The bloom of his youth, the roundness of his adolescent belly under the foppish satin smallclothes he had then affected, had long since gone. His figure had grown gaunt, his sloping shoulders stooped; his face, small for his height, was colorless, almost gray under his ceremonial white wig; his long nose was pinched, and his large hazel eyes looked up from his papers with an expression of anxiety.

Across the table he met the level blue gaze of a man who was ruddy of countenance and stocky of build, but who kept his fingers interlocked to control their trembling. Anyone, however, who tried to connect the shaking of Sam Adams's hands with weakness of character would have made the same mistake as one who read infirmity of purpose into the sensitive look about the Governor's eyes. Both were men of courage and tenacity. Adam's affliction was a palsy, peculiar to his family. It had been growing on him since his return from his long, thankless drudgeries in Continental Congress; by now it was so bad that he had all but renounced the pen with which he had roused his state to its stand against the king. He wrote only letters now, and few of these because the effort was painful and they must be copied by his daughter before being sent. He could, however, with no loss of honor have sent his own first drafts. Though each character was formed of a dozen quivering strokes, so steely was the purpose that directed the faltering hand that the general line showed firm and clear.

Had the disaffected of Worcester and Hampshire counties known that Sam Adams was now sitting on the Governor's councils, they would have been reassured, for surely he, if anyone in Boston, was one of them. It was primarily his writings that had nerved them down the path of Revolution; to be sure, they may not have known it, for Sam assumed a dozen literary disguises: Cotton Mather, Alfred, Impartialist, Candidus. They were better acquainted with his part in forming the committees of correspondence and the county conventions that had so effectively controlled the early course of the Revolution. To him they owed their technique of taking a stand against a newer oppression in a manner both forceful and orderly. They were grateful to him for having shown them how, and he could not fail to appreciate the thoroughness with which they had learned their lesson.

He was their man in other ways. If they were poor, so was Sam. "I glory in being what the world calls a poor man," he had written his wife, Betsy. Though he now sat in the hated Senate, given the property required for membership there, it was a puzzle to know how he qualified. He was not one of those who had fattened themselves at the public charge; his friends said that he would have been better rewarded if he had devoted his life to the digging of clams instead of to the public service.

He had been acquainted since youth with privation. Entering Harvard fifth in his class, a rank based on his family standing in the social hierarchy, not on scholarship, he had remained to graduate only by resorting to menial tasks like waiting tables. His degradation had been caused by his father's investments in the Land Bank, an institution designed to alleviate hard times in the 1740's by issuing paper money against holdings in real estate. Currently the farmers were looking for just such a measure. Adams must understand them, he whose quarrel with Thomas Hutchinson, and by extension with King George of England, had originated in Hutchinson's smashing of this humanitarian measure and with it the Adams fortune.

There were even more striking parallels between the situations. After the death of Sam's father, the law had tried to attach the homestead on Purchase Street and the brewery that Sam continued to operate after a fashion. Exactly as farmers in western Massachusetts had been banding together to stand off constables bent on seizing their cattle for debts and taxes, so Sam had stood off the Boston authorities, and had prevailed.

When Sam had risen to office and had become Boston tax-collector, he was a tax-collector after their own hearts. He was no man to grind the faces of the poor in times of distress; his office had coincided with such calamities as the fire of 1760 and the smallpox epidemic of 1764. Sheer neighborly reluctance to press for payment under painful circumstances and clumsy attempts to juggle accounts by applying the collections of a new year to the delinquencies of the last had got him into a scandal that had enabled

Hutchinson to brand him as "defaulting tax collector."
Boston had not held him too strictly to account; western
Massachusetts asked only that God send them such a col-
lector.

The troubled farmers of the outer counties had a more
personal reason to think warmly of Sam Adams. He had
been one of the committee of three sent by General Court
in 1782 into Hampshire County to give a hearing to the
grievances that had led to the outbreak under the roving
agitator Ely. Probably he had on that occasion said less
than his fellow committeemen, Artemas Ward and Nathaniel Gorham. Sam Adams was not a man to say much
in public, partly because the palsy in his arm was matched
by a quavering in his voice, which he could control only
when he raised it to lead psalm-singing in Sabbath meeting. If he could have sung a public discourse, he would
have been a magnificent orator; since this was not customary, Sam worked behind scenes, composing the orations
that men of better stage presence delivered.

His contribution to public discussions was inconspicuous
but often decisive. "Let him finish," he would say quietly,
when the crowd tried to shout down an uncouth speaker.
Then the speaker, heartened by the attentive regard of so
distinguished a man, would begin to make sense. The
crowd would discover that the untutored orator was on
the side of the angels — that is, of Sam Adams; or if he
were not, that his fuller explanation threw so ridiculous a
light on his reasoning that rebuttal was superfluous.

Thanks to such guidance, the Hatfield convention of
August 1782, begun stormily, ended in reconciliation. Its
resolutions stressed loyalty to government even above
grievances, and ended in a tribute to the committee for the
"patient, friendly, and generous attention with which they

have heard our various reports." The tribute had not
singled out Sam, but he got the most credit; he had been
the best listener.

The time had come to listen to them again; more than
anything the farmers needed a hearing. After all, they
had, from their point of view, done nothing outrageous.
The events in Northampton and Worcester had been accompanied by a minimum of rudeness; no one had suggested knocking the gray wigs off the judges, as once had
the egregious Ely. They had used bayonets on Judge
Ward, but they hadn't run him through, and when the
man had insisted on speaking, they had listened. They
needed Sam Adams to listen to them.

At the moment Sam was listening to Governor Bowdoin.

2.

The Governor's emergency board had been meeting
daily since Thursday, September 7, when he had summoned it to discuss the bad news from Worcester. The
full report demonstrated that the proclamation of September 2 had been so much wind. The mutinous spirit
abroad would not be quelled by mere words; friends to
government would not oppose it for fear of reprisal.
Three more courts impended on September 12 in Middlesex, Berkshire, and Bristol counties, all of them heavily
disaffected. What did the board advise the Governor to do
to protect them?

The board deliberated, slept on the problem, and on
Friday came to a decision. The Governor must act before
the mobs did; when court assembled, the militia must
assemble with it and stand by to protect the judges. But
this solution only landed them in a fresh quandary. The
Governor had a report from the commanding officer in

Middlesex that he could not guarantee that his men would muster in response to such orders.

Well then, Bowdoin's advisers said indignantly, he must call on the loyal militia of loyal counties to march against the disloyal. Was that legal? someone nervously asked. On that question the emergency board hung over to Saturday, when its legal talent gave its opinion; the Governor had authority to send the militia of any county wherever it was needed. Accordingly, two Suffolk companies of artillery, from Dorchester and Roxbury respectively, were ordered out to Concord.

Sam Adams made no protest; the necessity was too obvious. But to send armed men from one county to regulate the affairs of another was setting a bitter precedent. There were other solutions, and Sam remembered them. He spent Saturday morning in Boston town meeting and put himself on a committee appointed to draft an appeal to the malcontents. It would contain his best eloquence. After service in the Old South Church, after his usual Sunday dinner of baked beans and brown bread kept warm since the night before in the brick oven, he resumed work on the appeal, and was thus occupied when the summons came from the Governor.

This time Bowdoin had good news. Concord also had held town meeting on Saturday, and its members had registered unanimous disapproval of the "disorderly proceedings" in Worcester and Hampshire counties. They had sent out a call to other Middlesex towns to help them restrain the reckless. The restraint was to be exercised through a county convention to open in Concord on Monday, the day before court, if possible, or at the latest on Tuesday. Its members would discuss constitutional means of redressing grievances, and if any "designing men" came to make trouble for court, they would dissuade them.

With prayerful relief the Governor's board heard these details. Far better to let Concord control Concord than to send in the Dorchester artillery. Even Sam Adams forgot his prejudice against conventions, since the purpose of this one was righteous. He added his voice to the others, to countermand the order to the militia, and with renewed fervor went home to complete Boston's appeal to the fretful little towns upstate.

3.

Concord, however, had promised what Concord could not deliver. Concord's intentions were wholly virtuous, but Concord was not Middlesex County. There were other towns. There were, for instance, Harvard and Shirley and Groton, and in all of these places lived some very determined men.

Harvard was currently best known for its colony of what were called the "Shaking Quakers." Farmers from miles around borrowed each other's teams to drive in and watch them at their singing and dancing and speaking with tongues. The Shakers were not out to stop courts; they were too glad of their protection, for in earlier times Harvard people had done worse than gape at them. The Shakers had responded to the grievances of the world by withdrawing from it. To them had repaired many of the lowly: the poor who but for the colony might have suffered the indignity of becoming public charges; the aged who gratefully renounced the temptations of the flesh.

In Harvard also lived one of the mighty, Brigadier General Josiah Whitney. He no longer commanded the Middlesex militia, but he was one of the reasons that it would not march. Whitney had a low opinion of the Court of Common Pleas and expressed it freely.

In near-by Shirley, Nathan Smith was marshaling his

neighbors for a march on Concord. He was rough-man-
nered, hard-drinking, and maimed, not from the Revolutionary battles in which he had taken part, but in a pugil-
istic bout which had cost him an eye.

His neighbor, James Parker, watched him go and made
note of the fact in the almanac in which he recorded his
observations of life in his community. Parker was something of a scholar, and not only took his turn teaching the
winter session of the district school, but had a daughter
Sally who also taught. To this end he worked over his
fanciful spelling, recording a farm implement variously
as sithe, sith, until he somehow triumphantly fastened on
scythe.

Parker was one of those veterans who, having promptly
answered the call to Lexington, as promptly went home
again and stayed there. Having spent the war minding his
own business, and being one who got what "foreign superfluities" he craved by indefatigable swapping instead of
going into debt for them, he enjoyed a modest prosperity
and did not follow Nathan Smith to court. On the other
hand, he had no inclination at all to stop him. All unwittingly "Jam" Parker was an important factor in the turbulence overtaking Massachusetts, one of the many who
looked on with benevolent neutrality if not outright sympathy while others took action. There were more James
Parkers than Nathan Smiths, and they were more incor-
rigible. Governor Bowdoin would presently be driven to
explicit denunciation of Parker's kind, hold their passivity
responsible for the excesses of the others, but he might
better have saved his breath. Nathan Smith might repent;
James Parker never.

In Groton, stirring about on his preparations for court,
Parker had a friend who was to become more famous than
any insurgent heard from so far. He was Captain Job

Shattuck. Like Adam Wheeler, he was a veteran of two wars, and in his fifties he had more muscle, staying-power, and sheer audacity than most men in their twenties. Already he had made some stir against government, in 1781, when he had led a riot against the Silver Tax. A fine of £50 had not cowed him, and he felt no shame at having taken a stand against what he deemed injustice, nor did his friends feel it for him.

Now he was out to take another stand and willing to let the whole world know it. There would be in Concord none of that unseemly shrinking from leadership that had marred the Worcester proceedings. He would lead. And if writing was called for, Job Shattuck would write his name as large as John Hancock's on the Declaration and put it there with as much pride.

4.

Concord town meeting had hoped to have its convention in full session by Monday. To that end its riders had been circulating the county as industriously as ever had Paul Revere, and with general success, for twenty-seven towns sent delegates. But a call to peace seldom has the force of a call to arms. Few delegates managed to reach Concord before Tuesday; the "designing men" whom they hoped to restrain were more forehanded.

Toward noon on Monday the first arrivals at the convention looked out from Clark's Tavern to see the invaders come in. The Groton detachment under Job Shattuck came first, and hard on their heels the Shirley men, led by Nathan Smith, who, with his fighter's build and the patch over one eye, looked like everyone's notion of a pirate. Their followers, men and boys, numbered at least a hundred, and many were armed.

More ominous than their numbers was the thorough-

ness of their preparations. Shattuck came up the road at
the head of a lurching caravan of carts and wagons,
drawn by as many horses and oxen as he could press into
service. He had with him several loads of hay, wagons
piled high with posts and sawn boards, messes of provision, and several kegs of rum. Such forethought beto-
kened more than a demonstration; Shattuck was prepared
to lay all Concord under siege.

Some men left the tavern and went into the square to
begin their mission of dissuasion, but Job had no time for
them. The unloading of the caravan required his full attention. He was engaged in nothing less than the setting
up of camp on Concord Green; under his direction the
poles were being hammered into the ground, the boards
placed across them, and hay spread on the ground beneath. Job was digging in for heavy weather.

During the night it came. Thanks perhaps to Judge
Ward's imprecations at Worcester, the skies opened and
poured down on Concord. The rain drove through the in-
secure shelters on the green, and some men left the damp
hay and took refuge in neighboring barns and the courthouse itself, and everyone broached the kegs of rum. By
the time court was due to assemble on Tuesday it was the
opinion of most observers that Job's army was too drunk
to know why it was there.

But, wet or dry, Job himself was not one to forget what
he was about. He went about camp keeping his men in
some sort of order, turned a deaf ear to emissaries from
the convention, and watched the road from the west.

Early in the afternoon the cause of his westering gaze
became apparent. The insurgents did not share the government's compunctions about riding from one county to
the next. At two o'clock the reinforcements came in, and
at their head rode what in the downpour looked like the

Knight of the Doleful Countenance, Adam Wheeler of Hubbardston.

Observers from the convention noted other details, for though this body was now in full session and had moved to the more capacious quarters of the meetinghouse, the racket in the square made it difficult for them to concentrate on their deliberations. They saw that though the newcomers were armed, their muskets had taken such a drenching that there was little likelihood that they could be fired. Still, the waterlogged muskets would have utility as clubs, and the bayonets were impervious to weather.

The onlookers noted a further alarming circumstance. The newcomers included men not only from Wheeler's Worcester County, but from Hampshire; they could be recognized by their blue-checked shirts, a specialty of the Connecticut Valley, and by the fact that Captain Hinds of Greenwich rode at Wheeler's side. Thus far had the organization of anarchy carried.

But anarchy was not the objective of Captain Wheeler. At the entrance to town he dressed his ranks, ordered the drums to beat, and resumed the march to the courthouse with a solemn dignity that moved even Sheriff Loammi Baldwin to admiration.

It was Nathan Smith in the courthouse square who stood for anarchy. Smith, very wet, not impossibly very drunk, or perhaps unable in the rain to distinguish with his one eye between friend and foe, gave the newcomers a rough welcome.

With "high oaths," according to Baldwin, he advanced upon Wheeler, declaring that "every person who did not follow his men and join the Regulators should be driven out of town at the point of the bayonet."

"You take back them words!" said Wheeler. He hadn't

led his friends these many miry miles to suffer indignities
like these.

Smith, nudged by Job Shattuck, took back "them
words," and the companies united. By three the leaders
had drafted a message which Job Shattuck signed and carried in person to the convention to be relayed to the
judges: "The voice of the People of this county is that
[the court] shall not enter this courthouse until such time
as the People shall have redress of the grievances they
labor under at present."

The judges, owing to the "badness of the weather,"
had not assembled a quorum until one, and had since made
no attempt to marshal a procession to the beleaguered
courthouse. They sat in Jones Tavern, looking out lugu-
briously into the rain, and waiting for the convention, under whose protection Governor Bowdoin seemed to have
put them, to restore order. But the best efforts of the convention had elicited only this.

The "insolence" of the ultimatum "wounded the feelings of every gentleman," reproachfully wrote Judge
Samuel P. Savage to a Governor who had denied his
judges the aid and comfort of the Suffolk County militia.
What, asked the judges of the committee from the convention, should they do? Deprecatingly the committee
thought they had best adjourn as requested. Would the
committee, asked the judges, take the sense of the convention on that? Back came the word from the convention:
the judges should adjourn.

The judges drafted a statement that since they "as justices of the court were held in duress by a body of men in
arms they neither would nor could act," and asked that it
be read to the mob. The committee respectfully declined.
The mob, it pointed out, might well pull down the court-

house if irritated. The judges gave up. In the privacy of their tavern they went through the face-saving move of opening court and adjourning it, this time not without day but to November.

The convention consoled them with a resolution (also not very publicly proclaimed) expressing "utter abhorrence of the means adopted by the body at arms." But the convention had wanted exactly what the mob had, and had been in any case impotent to save the judges from humiliation. If the Governor did not approve the conduct of the latter, what, their message to him asked, would he have had them do?

The men of the court, of the convention, and of Job's army took themselves home, some of the latter to hot mustard poultices and flannel bandages. Concord was free again, except for the litter of trampled hay and poles abandoned on the green. For days after, small boys resorted there to re-enact the drama of the court. "I'm a Regulator," said one side, and stuck a sprig of hemlock in their caps. "I'm a government," said the other, and stuck white paper in theirs. For the insurgents, disliking that term, disliking even more to be called mob, had lately found a name for themselves; they were Regulators, and they had their insigne, a sprig of hemlock.

CHAPTER V

Judges

The efforts of the peacemakers in Concord, in which Bowdoin had placed his faith, had not been blessed. From the two other courts scheduled for the same day at opposite ends of the state, the news was little more reassuring. The courts were in Great Barrington for Berkshire County, and in Taunton for Bristol. One of them indeed was successfully defended, but it was not Bowdoin's ideal of civil government that it should be possible only under armed guard.

He had reason to hope for order in Berkshire County, for though it had held a convention, its resolutions had been surprisingly moderate, had even denounced the widespread agitation for paper money. This impression was, however, illusory. Those resolutions had passed only because conservative Berkshire citizens, unlike their counterparts elsewhere, instead of boycotting the convention, had managed to pack it.

The people at large, or at least a great many of them, were as furious against a government which had placed such burdens on them as any people anywhere. Some of them were turning on the constitution itself, were demanding that it be revised, or even annulled.

Berkshire County was something of a special case, the nearest Massachusetts still had to a frontier. Even the oldest of the towns along the Housatonic—Great Barrington, Stockbridge, Lenox—were very young, and the village of Adams near Mount Greylock had incorporated during the Revolution and named itself as a compliment to Sam. There were settlements known vaguely to Boston as "a place called Eleven Thousand Acres," valleys full of ghostly gray groves in the process of being cleared by the wastful and dangerous method of girdling. The last of the Indians had left only a year ago; they were only the praying Indians of Stockbridge, long domesticated by the missions, but one need not be old to remember wilder Indians and wilder ways.

Berkshire courts had been the first to close during the Revolution and the last to reopen. The county, whose leaders and not merely the People, had objected to the state's turning to the last royal charter even as a temporary makeshift, had all but seceded from the rest of the state in protest, and had hinted darkly at transferring its allegiance elsewhere: "There are others who would have us, bad as we are." Not until the ratification of the constitution of 1780 did the county resume its normal place in the commonwealth and permit the reopening of the civil courts. The people, who considered that they had got along very well without them, were the more shocked by the pressure of claims so old that they had been forgotten. All very well for gentry who had money and could take advantage of the situation. "I live in the midst of those who owe," one of the latter wrote complacently, "and shall be a considerable landowner in a little time."

It was a viewpoint not appreciated by those whose possessions were forfeit. Already Berkshire men had banded together to stand off the sheriff. Now they did not pro-

pose to defend their rights with less zeal than their neighbors to the east. They were ready for rough going.

Yet when Sheriff Caleb Hyde, in response to the Governor's orders, called out the militia to defend court, the
militia actually came. The courthouse square was already
crowded with men and boys armed with guns and bludgeons. But the militia, fully armed, and under the command
of the county's most distinguished soldier, General John
Paterson, numbered nearly a thousand, and could make
short work of clearing the square.

But the mind of the militia, it speedily transpired, was
divided as to the uses to which its services should be put.
There was such altercation in the ranks that when the
judges arrived, the chief justice suggested, with what
sounded like the wisdom of Solomon, that the general
divide his men: those who favored the sitting of the court
to the right of the road, those against to the left.

With this amicable, strictly republican suggestion General Paterson complied with what some people deemed
suspicious alacrity. The result: nearly eight hundred of
the militia took the left or contrary-minded side of the
road; less than two hundred the right. After such division
any message expressing the voice of the People was superfluous. The judges adjourned without day.

It had been almost too easy. The men who had taken
the trouble to guard the courthouse all night sought further outlet. One group followed the judges to the home of
the chief justice and demanded that they sign a pledge that
they would sit no more on the Court of Common Pleas
until General Court reassembled. The chief justice cheerfully obliged, his colleagues less cheerfully, all but Jahleel
Woodbridge, who snapped that he would resign his commission first.

The dissenter was not molested. The crowd had found

a new diversion. Happily they went back to the square and
stormed their own bastille. They broke open the county
jail and set all the debtors free. Then everyone went home
to chores.

Oddly enough, Sheriff Hyde made no report on the
leadership of the insurgents. If those Berkshire men soon
to become famous as principals in the "rebellion" were
here today, their presence went unmarked, except for one
Thomas Rust, a middle-aged cordwainer, who would have
a hand in nearly everything of a subversive character that
ensued in Berkshire County. The fact was that the conduct
of lesser men was eclipsed by scandalously manifest sympathy from the chief justice himself.

He was Judge William Whiting. When he wasn't sitting on the bench, he rode about the county with his medicine bags as country doctor. In that capacity he had perhaps closer acquaintance with the miseries of the people
than most judges, and he was all for them. "I have never
heard anybody point out a better way to have their grievances redressed than the people have taken," he was saying. "If the law had gone on two years longer in the way
it has done, the common people would all be slaves."

To such views, shocking in an officer of the commonwealth, Judge Whiting had given more than casual expression; he had put them in writing. In a series of articles
to which he signed himself as "Grachus," he restated with
something of the force of a Berkshire Sam Adams the
complaints of the people. He attacked the redemption of
the securities, saying that the veterans, who must now pay
twenty shillings in taxes for every two they had received,
might better have served without pay. He protested that
court fees were ruining poor debtors in a situation where
the people were "almost universally indebted to each
other."

He wrote his own declaration of independence. "People ought to know that it is the indispensable duty of the people at large in all free republican governments to guard their liberties," he declared. When crafty men try to enslave the people, "it is a virtue in them to disturb the government."

These were memorable sentiments in a judge, and in time to come remembered they were. Far from concealing his opinions, Judge Whiting circulated his "Grachus" articles industriously. They fell into the hands of a still more eminent Berkshire man, Theodore Sedgwick, just back from a tour of duty with Continental Congress. Sedgwick replied in detail and saw to it that Governor Bowdoin knew what kind of chief justice he had in Berkshire County.

2.

Bristol County, for the peace of mind of the commonwealth, had a very different sort of judge. He was Judge David Cobb, who was also General David Cobb, commander of the Bristol County militia. "I'll sit as judge or die in my boots as general," he said as the day of Taunton Court approached.

As general he called out the militia, not only that of Bristol County, whose sympathies might be suspect, but of Plymouth County, and with this force he occupied the courthouse before the mob could. On the day before court, Governor Bowdoin, apparently as scared by the judge's militance as by that of the insurgents, got a cautionary message to him: the militia was to be employed only if there was actual danger of bloodshed. Judge Cobb hardly anticipated that. No one else had shed blood; why should Bristol County? But he judged that the Governor had spoken too late and went on with his plans.

As he expected, a few hundred men, sketchily armed, presented themselves before Taunton courthouse. They made no demonstration; they merely waited to see what would happen. What happened pleased them. In the courthouse the general, assuming his character as judge, decided in consultation with his colleagues to be generous. If the people didn't want court, why force it on them? Court adjourned of its own free will to the second Tuesday in December.

"A generous concession on the part of authority!" shouted the mob; at least Judge Cobb, who lacked perhaps a nice ear for idiom, said that they so shouted.

The mob hung around for a while, reluctant as the farmers of Berkshire to let a great day go by so tamely; then at dusk they began to disperse.

"Good night," some of them called out cheerfully as they passed their friends in the militia.

"Good night," the militia called back.

That was the tone of things at this place, at this time.

3.

In a purely physical sense the mode of the rebellion — if that was what Massachusetts was having — had so far been remarkably innocuous, especially compared to the still recent riots in Boston preceding the Revolution, the house-wreckings, the tea-dumping, to say nothing of the Boston Massacre. Guns had been carried, yet not one had gone off, even by accident; bayonets had been fixed, but no one had been run through. Lawbreakers the newly embattled farmers might be, but they had shown nevertheless remarkable forbearance.

This viewpoint was impressed upon the readers of Boston's *Independent Chronicle* by "A Contented Subject." "In America mobs are noisy and stop courts — in Great

Britain they are riotous and pull down houses. In England or Ireland a man is liable in the most peaceful times to be robbed at noon. In America any man is safe at midnight in the largest cities and surrounded with a Hampshire convention or a Worcester mob."

It was a thought, but Governor Bowdoin found little comfort in it. Government by mobs, however orderly, was no government at all, and government was what he was sworn to uphold. He couldn't do it singlehanded. General Court must come back to help him. It must pass on what these people called grievances, make concessions where concessions were reasonable and just, and, above all, back his efforts to restore order.

A new legislative session had been one of the demands of the disaffected. If he granted it, the people were bound to wait patiently on its deliberations.

But General Court had to be summoned; it couldn't be pulled out of a hat. It was past the middle of September before Bowdoin sent out the call, and nearly the end of the month before it could assemble. In the meantime events kept on happening, and some of them were frightening.

There was, for instance, the response to the address of Boston town meeting to the people of Massachusetts on which Sam Adams (with the aid of a distinguished committee) had spent so many hours and all his subtle knowledge of propaganda.

It opened with consummate tact. To have begun with a scolding would have hardened the farmers in their conviction that Boston was the purse-proud contriver of all their woes. So the address began with a disarming reminder of the time when Boston, under siege by the British, its poor starving, had been a suppliant for charity, and of the generosity with which upstate towns had responded to the bundles-for-Boston movement, sending corn and beeves and pork. Warmly Boston gave thanks again.

It was now Boston's turn to repay that debt by helping the rest of the state to remove the evils under which it suffered. But this must be done in a lawful way, and under the constitution which the people had engaged to obey for fifteen years. During the Revolution the breaking of the tie with Britain had forced the people into a "state of nature." Such a condition, however unavoidable then, was productive of endless conflict. The people now had the General Court to resolve their grievances, and if one session failed to do so, "we can in the next election place men in power who will answer to our reasonable expectations." But the expectations must be reasonable and the principle accepted that the will of the majority must be obeyed.

The sympathetic tone, the general tact of the address was marred by an irritating reference to "the habits of luxury contracted in the late war" as the real cause of the present troubles, and a suggestion that the people had not acted of themselves but under pressure from foreign agents, "British emissaries residing among us, whose every wish is for overthrow or ruin."

Even so, the appeal was eloquent, but Adams had forgotten what he should have learned in 1782 when he went personally to Hampshire County to reason with the disaffected. He had succeeded less by much speaking than by patient listening; the disaffected had been given not a scolding but a hearing. Now as the address circulated in Hampshire, peppery little Greenwich retorted that Boston, far from listening to grievances, didn't even recognize their existence.

The allusion to luxuries and British emissaries caused the Greenwich town fathers to mix metaphors in their fury. "Example is stronger than precept," they replied. "We pray you to consider what feeling the young and tender breast must be possessed of when his own eyes see his elder brother clothed in purple . . . and the younger obliged to submit to the coarsest fare and hard toil, clothed in rags and yet belonging to the same family." British emissaries were unknown in Greenwich, but "we have been concerned for Boston on account of so many of these emissaries being so cordially received and so kindly entertained as . . . they have been in that town."

And why, Greenwich inquired, with ominous logic, should Boston object to the means taken to redress inequities when they were the same that Boston itself had once taught and taken "when our grievances ware less real and more ideal than they are now"?

No one can speak that way to Boston. Boston's revenge would come late, but it would be like the judgment on Gomorrah. Its audacious little enemy on the plain would be blotted from the map, only its hilltops showing as islets above the floods gathered up together to give Boston its water supply. That was long after, and Sam Adams had no hand in it, and though it was a judgment bitterly contested by Greenwich, the more ancient quarrel was by then no longer remembered. But had the Greenwich of 1786 been told what was in store, it would not have been surprised; it would have put nothing past Boston.

4.

Meanwhile the trouble in Massachusetts was spilling across the borders. Rhode Island was in turmoil. It was a different sort of turmoil because in Rhode Island the insurgents — that is to say, the debtors — were in control of the legislature, and it was the creditors who were in rebellion. The state offered the novel spectacle of debtors in full pursuit of their creditors, trying to force on them cash for payment in full.

The cash was the new paper-money emission put into the pockets of the debtors by state loans, and the creditors were resisting, were in fact leaving the state to avoid taking it. The merchants were closing their doors. The farmers, as bewildered by this state of affairs as were their brothers in Massachusetts, were passing legislation to enforce heavy penalties on creditors and merchants who refused to take good paper cash.

Nothing that happened in Rhode Island was the result of events in Massachusetts. It was rather in the eyes of Boston a horrible example of what would happen in the Bay State if the likes of Luke Day, Adam Wheeler, Job Shattuck, and Judge William Whiting had their way.

The bad example of Massachusetts was, however, directly responsible for an alarming incident in New Hampshire. On September 20 several hundred armed men surrounded the Legislature in Exeter and proposed to lay it under siege until it yielded to their demands for a remission of taxes and an issue of paper money.

The New Hampshire chief executive, called president in those parts, was that General John Sullivan whose fame extended into the Carolinas. Like Artemas Ward in Worcester, he contemptuously pushed the bayonets aside and lectured the mob on their folly; and with better effect, for his very composure gave credence to a rumor that a company of artillery was on the way to support him. The mob took flight, and Sullivan, who had no compunction about resorting to arms when necessary, called out the guard and had them pursued.

The incident had a dual effect in Massachusetts. Some envied New Hampshire its possession of a chief executive capable of such brisk action. Others were panic-stricken by the fact that a mob could grow so bold as to attack such high authority. What had happened yesterday in Exeter might happen tomorrow in Boston.

It was unfortunate for the peace of mind of officials in Essex County that less than a week later the Court of Common Pleas was due to sit, not in Salem, which would have been safe, but in Newburyport, hardly more than a stone's throw from the New Hampshire border. There was this time no argument about calling out the militia; it was called, and even under its protection the judges were nervous, hustling through their business with unseemly speed.

Nothing at all happened. True, some members of the militia heard rude remarks. A captain was told apropos of future developments: "You'll be the first man I shoot." But there was no rioting, and the artillery was put to it to fill up its time by giving an exhibition on the training-field. Here for the first time blood was drawn, the first casualty incurred — "an innocent cow that . . . stepped into their path to fame."

But the quiet in Newburyport was not matched in Hampshire County, where on the same day was taking place that which would cause General Court to open its session under a cloud, bring the Secretary of War to Massachusetts for an alarmed tour of inspection, and, as not the least of results, give the Massachusetts insurgents what they had so far lacked — a leader.

CHAPTER VI

The Celebrated Captain Shays

It is no insult to the memory of a likable, honorable, and courageous gentleman to say that in Daniel Shays the insurgents hadn't found much of a leader. It was a distinction that he didn't ask for or pretend to, and in fact strenuously denied.

"I their leader? I am not!" said Captain Shays.

Those were not the words of a dictator; they weren't even very brave words. The truth is that though Shays entered the movement of his own free will, he stayed with it for the same reason that a man stays with a tiger he has elected to ride; he couldn't get off. And since a man in that predicament is bound to be conspicuous, leadership was thrust on him.

There was little formality involved. Both sides consciously and unconsciously were looking for some sort of focus to the strange forces that were convulsing Massachusetts. The one was talking of "artful and designing men"; the other, to judge by satires in the *Hampshire Gazette,* which began publication in Northampton in the exciting days of early September and rushed into the fray on the side of government, was looking for a Robin Hood. When Shays appeared, arriving late but undeniably in charge of the boldest action thus far, he was seized upon

68

by both sides as the leader they had been looking for.

Friends to government saw in him the "artful, designing man" of their suspicions; newspapers, ignoring the
men who had led the inception of the movement, took
pains to collect anecdotes about Shays. The people took
him to their hearts, or at least they took his name; the
greenwood would presently ring with their rallying cry:
"Hurrah for Daniel Shays!"

If the rebellion lacked its Robin Hood, one had to be
invented. Upon an obscure captain of the Continental
Army, now a dirt farmer in Pelham, was visited the fate
of popular leaders; he became less a man than a myth.

2.

When the Revolution broke out, Daniel Shays, though
pushing thirty, had not even a farm of his own. He had
been born to poverty, had had to scratch for a living since
early boyhood, and had worked as a hired man in Brookfield. But he was a superior hand, hard-working, depend-
able, and he got superior pay. After hours his recreation
was as vigorous as his work in the fields; he drilled men
and boys on the village green in the manual of arms,
equipping some of them with sticks for want of muskets.
After the call to Lexington, Brookfield saw no more of
him, except once when he returned on recruiting duty and,
in anticipation of a commission, took the opportunity to
marry Abigail Gilbert. Already he had distinguished himself for gallantry in action at Bunker Hill. Later he
served at Saratoga and Stony Point. For a brief time he
was under the command of the illustrious Lafayette;
somewhere he had been wounded, and even his enemies
would always acknowledge him to be a "tolerable good
soldier" and steady under fire.

But there were two counts against him of which his

enemies now made much. One was the means by which he
got his commission. He had driven a Yankee bargain to
get it, they said, enlisting men, once his first quota was
filled, on the understanding that they would serve under
him as captain. Such an arrangement was anything but un-
usual in Massachusetts. Washington, a firm believer in
the hierarchy of rank, had been afflicted when he arrived
in Cambridge by the neighborly practice by which men in
the ranks elected their own officers and refused to re-enlist
unless they could be sure of having the officer of their
choice.

What, Massachusetts men inquired, was wrong with
the custom? Where does honor lie, with the fine British
gentleman who with no knowledge of the service buys
himself a commission, or with the Yankee soldier of hard-
bitten experience who wins it by calling men to rise up and
follow? Shays nevertheless had to fight long and hard to
carry his point, and when in 1779 he finally got his commission, retroactive to January 1777, he was not very well
received by his fellow officers. But his men were content,
and with them he was at home in the comradeship of the
camp until a new difficulty arose.

This was the familiar difficulty of keeping body and
soul together without pay, or with pay so heavily depreci-
ated as to be nearly worthless. The trouble came to a
head in 1780 when Washington, aware that his subalterns
were resigning in droves, bitterly told Continental Congress that if the officers of the army "are retiring from the
field to grow old in poverty, wretchedness and contempt
. . . I shall have learned what ingratitude is. . . . I
shall have realized a tale which will embitter every moment of my future life."

Officers who remained in the service were sometimes
put to quaint devices to turn a penny. A chivalrous young

officer of Burgoyne's captive army had been scandalized
to see a Massachusetts brigadier pull the boots off his feet
when one of his prisoners offered a guinea for them. And
Shays's officers were more than scandalized, they were
outraged, when he sold his sword. They even talked of
court-martialing him for conduct unbecoming an officer
and a gentleman.

Well, why not? asked Shays. The sword was rightfully
his and not picked up in plunder like some articles he could
mention. Since he had come by it he had two swords, and
no officer, however exalted his rank, goes into action with
a sword at either hip. He had preserved the blade that
meant the most to him, the one he had carried at Stony
Point. The one he had sold was what the newspapers
called a "foreign superfluity."

The trouble was that it had been given him, and by no
less a person than the young Marquis de Lafayette.
Newly returned from France, he had brought with him a
quantity of "elegant swords" to present to American officers. One of these had gone to Shays, and this was the
one Shays had sold.

There was justice in the wrath of Shays' colleagues. A
sword from Lafayette was no chattel to be disposed of to
meet the vulgar needs of the belly. Not even George
Washington, who understood the need so well, would
have forgiven so shabby an expedient.

Smarting, but with head held high, in October 1780
Shays resigned his commission and went home. He settled
in Pelham, and had been there ever since.

3.

Pelham was Scotch-Irish. The term was only vaguely
understood in some parts of Massachusetts, still Puritan
enough to believe that anything with Irish connections,

however hyphenated, was bound to be Papist. For this reason the founders of Pelham had been driven out of Worcester, where they had first settled; the town had grudgingly suffered them until they undertook to erect a meetinghouse. Its services would have been as orthodox as any under the ancient theocracy, but Worcester, partly because it was costive about permission to set up separate congregations, and partly because it would stomach no meetinghouse with Irish overtones, had torn the building down, and the builders had indignantly gone off to Pelham.

That had been nearly a half-century ago. Since then the Scotch-Irish had flourished, had commanded respect for their community. Their town was in the hills; their fields were less fruitful than the rich bottom lands of the Connecticut Valley; the soil was rather thin, having been burned over too often by hunters, Indian and white, and drought sometimes bore down hard on acres too high for the fetching of water.

Nevertheless, in the main and until recently they had prospered. Their women had the respect of the Valley for the skill with which they raised their flax and spun it on wheels ingeniously turned by foot. Their farmers had done much to educate the Valley to the raising of potatoes, hitherto considered fit only for hogs or the Irish. Even good families ate potatoes now.

There was still some tendency to laugh at Pelham when opportunity offered. The town had laid itself open to ridicule not long ago when it had opened its pulpit to the young "Reverend Davis," who turned out to be no Reverend and no Davis, but a nineteen-year-old scapegrace named Stephen Burroughs. When Pelham discovered the deception, its sending of a posse to Rutland in unsuccessful pursuit had evoked derision.

Even the later capture of Burroughs in Springfield and his conviction there for passing counterfeit money had been little comfort, for in jail Burroughs composed and delivered to all comers a lampoon on Pelham in what he called his "Hay Mow Sermon," and the whole county had laughed at Pelham's expense.

That mischance was now safely in the past. Since then Burroughs had made a monkey out of the Northampton jailer by setting fire to his quarters, of the commander of Castle Island in Boston Harbor by leading a temporarily successful jailbreak. Later when he had been induced to serve his term, he would bring derision on Worcester County's Charlton, where he would become famous as the only man in Massachusetts ever accused of attempting rape on horseback.

But now no one was laughing at Pelham, whose vigor in taking a stand against oppression commanded the completest respect.

4.

Shays himself, to this day, had taken no part in that stand. He had not remained aloof, for he was as much troubled by current difficulties as anyone. He had been haled to court for debt, though not to debtors' prison, and was said to have been roused to passionate protest when he saw the bed of a sick woman snatched from under her to satisfy a claim.

Nor was he aloof from community life. The Irish overtones of Pelham had an appeal for a man whose father had been a Patrick who sometimes spelled his surname as Sheas, and whose mother a Margaret Dempsey. The town had made him at home, had entered him in the records as "gent," not because he was of great estate — judging from a surviving photograph and a cellar hole, his

home in Conkey's Hollow on West Hill could hardly have
been more than two rooms — but because an officer is a
gentleman of course. It had made him town warden,
elected him delegate to some of the earlier Hampshire
conventions, and afforded him what was his dearest pleasure, the drilling of the local militia on the green.

Yet when in late August most of the Pelham company
had taken the road to Northampton, Daniel Shays had
stayed behind. He assuredly had not gone with it, for the
Pelham men arrived under the command of Captain
Hinds of Greenwich, and Sheriff Porter, taking careful
note of names, could not have missed Shays had he been
present. He knew the man and had seen him as recently
as Election Day, when Shays had led his company into
Hadley to give an exhibition. Yet when Pelham marched
on a much more serious mission, Shays, with whatever
pang in his heart, stood with the women to watch them
off.

"I told them it was inconsistent after we had agreed
to petition." He said that much later and in a different
context, but the remark explains his inactivity in August.
Shays looked on with none of the detachment of the
Shirley diarist James Parker, who had watched Nathan
Smith and Job Shattuck set off for Concord; his heart
was with them, their cause was his. But he held on for
a while to a conviction that they were going about it in the
wrong way. Indeed, he seems never to have lost it.

What now drew him into action of an incriminating
kind almost in spite of himself was a complex of motives.

"I could not withstand their importunities," was the
way he put it, for in spite of an underprivileged boyhood,
Shays had had a term or two at country school, and, like
most of the literate of his time, seldom put in one syllable
what five would express as well.

The remark referred to Pelham itself, to the close communal life, stifling at its worst, but deeply sustaining at its best, whereby no man lives unto himself alone. When a child is gravely ill in the Pelhams of the world, no mother is suffered to watch and grieve uncomforted. The women come in with broths and fresh linen; they pack the exhausted mother off to bed and take their turns sitting all night by the sickbed. The men, even the oldest and most dignified, stop the father on the streets to ask how it goes, and if it goes badly, their eyes mutely reflect the grief in his.

There can be enmities too, and division the more painful because it's as if the foot were at war with the head. An apprehension of so fatal, unnatural a division was growing in Massachusetts; it was a dread of contributing to it, rather than timidity, that had given men so different as Governor Bowdoin and Captain Shays their reluctance to take up arms.

But it wasn't in Shays to stay apart from his fellows. The current was too strong; there was in his town a passion for unity that was beyond him to withstand. His needs, his sympathies were one with his fellow townsmen's. He had been no laggard on the march to Lexington. How hold out now if he were needed?

Needed he was. The need grew out of an incident which passed almost without comment in the papers and was never connected by them with the sudden galvanizing of the insurgent spirit to really dangerous action. On September 19 the Supreme Judicial Court had met in Worcester, without molestation. It had not occurred to anyone to stop it. The quarrel of the farmers was with the civil Court of Common Pleas; with the Supreme Judicial Court, concerned with criminals, they had nothing to do. But it seemed they did. The court made criminals of

them, indicted eleven of their leaders on the charge of
being "disorderly, riotous and seditious persons" who
prevented "unlawfully and by force of arms . . . the
due execution of justice and the laws of the commonwealth." The indictments included many good friends of
Shays — Adam Wheeler of Hubbardston, Abraham and
Henry Gale of Princeton.

In Boston the phrase "condign punishment" was being bandied about. In untutored ears, especially those
who had caught some echo of Judge Ward's reference to
the gallows in his speech across the bayonets in Worcester,
"condign" sounded like a synonym for "capital."

The news roused the insurgents and their sympathizers
as they had not been roused before. What, treat as criminals decent men whose only crime had been to protect the
unfortunate? Call sedition that which, undertaken a
decade earlier by the same men, had been accounted purest
patriotism? Were the names of patriot and traitor mere
noises that their meanings could be glibly interchanged at
the convenience of gentlemen wearing wigs? Was it not
true patriotism to guard one's liberty jealously, and if it
were threatened by government itself, was it not, as a
humane judge had said, a virtue in the people to disturb
the government?

Even Shays felt that way. He had doubted the wisdom
of stopping court; that such action was criminal he could
not agree. Where was the justice in inflicting "condign
punishment" on men who, before leading their friends to
court to "entreat" it not to sit, ransacked Scripture and
prayed to God for guidance? Such a man was Adam
Wheeler, now put to uneasy dodges to escape the law; just
such another was Luke Day. And Luke Day would certainly be indicted in the session of the Supreme Judicial

Court in Springfield on September 26 if the judges had their way.

The judges must not have it. Not only in Hampshire County, for this was no local matter, but in Worcester and Berkshire men made their preparations, and as court Tuesday approached, as early as the Sunday before, they began to come to Springfield. Only a few were thus fore-handed, but there was word that at least two thousand were on their way, among them some well-wishers from Connecticut.

There was, the responsible realized, more danger than there had been before. It was not merely that the court was higher, but that so large and miscellaneous an assembly might easily degenerate into what their enemies called them, a mob. Not everyone would come prayer-fully. There would be lads itching for the excitement of knocking judges' heads together; there would be shifty-eyed men hoping under the cover of confusion to pick up a bit of plunder; most dangerous of all, because there were more of these, there would be honest men, fright-ened now, and in their fright desperate. For the dignity, for indeed the elementary safety of the cause, a firm leader was necessary, a man capable of keeping his head in an emergency and of holding the respect of the dis-orderly.

Daniel Shays was such a man. The very fact that he had until now taken no part in the popular movement qualified him the better for the task. He would command the respect of the judges themselves as a man acting purely in the public interest without selfish motive. They were good reasons, the situation was grave, and Shays was no coward. He set out for Springfield.

"I am so far from considering it a crime," said he later

of this venture, "that I look upon it that the government are indebted to me for what I did there."

5.

The Hampshire militia had recently become the charge of Major General William Shepard, who lived in Westfield, not far from Springfield, and knew well the temper of his county. He was alert, and the plans of the insurgents did not take him by surprise. Their impending march on Springfield imposed on him a double duty, not only of defending court, but of guarding the Federal arsenal, set up in town during the Revolution. Were the arsenal stores, its ammunition, stands of arms, artillery, to fall into insurgent hands, they would no more be the "despicable wretches" their enemies called them, but a formidable army.

Shepard was a humane man; the prospect of shedding the blood of good neighbors gave him nightmares, and, like Governor Bowdoin, he preferred conciliation to force. But the gravity of his responsibility left him little choice. It was for him to act before the insurgents could. As early as Saturday evening he put Sheriff Porter in charge of the courthouse with an armed guard of forty; by three o'clock Sunday morning he had him reinforced with two hundred of the Hampshire militia, men from Northampton and Hatfield. On Monday he called out more of the militia, and noting that some of them were of wavering sympathies, raised a band of some two hundred volunteers from the neighborhood of Springfield, arming them, with some shrinking at his own temerity, from the Federal stores.

When on Tuesday morning the insurgents came in force, they found the courthouse securely held and a small cannon mounted in front of it—"the government's puppy," the insurgents called it—and General Shepard in command of some nine hundred armed men. They themselves numbered at that stage little more than seven hundred, and less than a quarter were armed with anything better than clubs.

Undismayed, as composed as he always was in the context of purely physical action, Shays rode forward and saluted the general.

"Yes, general?" said Shepard.

"Captain, sir," Shays corrected him. He was proud of the rank he had fought the brass of the Continental Army to get; not even a major general should be permitted to mock it.

His men, said Captain Shays, desired to parade. Would the general retire his ranks sufficiently to permit them to do so?

It seemed a harmless request, even a wise precaution, to Shepard. Shays' men, having marched so far, could hardly be dismissed out of hand without being allowed some sort of demonstration. Ill-armed as they were, they posed no threat to the militia, and better that they were held to attention on parade than suffered to get restless and try out their clubs. Moreover, Shepard liked Shays, a subaltern of impeccable military manners.

Shays turned back to dress his ranks. His experience with the Continental Army had taught him how to put on a good front with meager resources. Such men of his little army as hadn't worn their old Continental uniform to rags, wore it today. He did himself, for he had kept his buff-and-blue with loving care, and his Abigail had polished its buttons. Most of his men had come in their ragged work clothes, but that had also been true of the

Continental Army. Shays had imposed uniformity by insisting that each man wear a sprig of evergreen in his cap.

To old soldiers looking on, the bits of green, hemlock by preference, brought a wrench of nostalgia. They were of honorable tradition; even so had Washington smartened up his ragged men when he had to make a show and nothing to do it with. General Shepard's militia, not notably better uniformed, had in this vein adopted a badge of their own, bits of white paper which they wore in their caps. But the force of the symbolism was with the hemlock. The paper was nondescript, without history, and easily lost in the wind.

Inspecting his ranks, the eye of Shays fell on young Henry McCullough of Pelham. The young man was without military or even insurgent experience; he had come along today mainly for the ride and also because he admired Shays. He was not even armed, but he rode a good horse. Shays moved him up forward, someone gave McCullough a cutlass, and so when the insurgent forces moved through the square in solemn procession, drums beating, fifes shrilling, nearly at their head, looking every inch the rebel commander, rode young Henry McCullough.

Shays' troops moved down the square in an order that even Shepard found admirable. The militia, watching in grave silence, was even more impressed than he. From time to time some of its members shook the white paper from their caps and, turning a stony back to reprimand, went into the square and fell in step with the marchers.

"A very sorrowful day," observed one onlooker, Jonathan Judd of Southampton, taking note of these defections. "Brother against brother, father against son."

Shays' army grew as it marched, not only by defections

from the militia, but by reinforcements from the country. The latter kept coming in all day, even after the parade had stopped and Shays had retired his men to Ferry Street and had gone apart to confer with a committee. They came in at night and the next day and the next. There was no country road for miles around without at least one party plodding in to Springfield, all prepared to stand up and be counted, and to take action if the judges didn't listen to reason.

The committee appointed to negotiate with the judges was made up of men who had no personal stake in their deliberations. Luke Day, for instance, was not among them, was not even mentioned as present. It must have gone against the grain for him to stay at home, but it was better strategy. Shays was delegated to approach the judges, carrying with him nothing more lethal than a petition.

The judges were this time not asked to suspend court, but only that part of its business that might affect the people currently in arms and those who had defended "their persons and property by preventing the Court of Common Pleas." The judges were, however, asked not to sit again until the grievances of the people had been redressed, and were also asked to dismiss the militia "without cost." Shays' committee had been making their own estimate of the number of the militia, the probable total of the pay due them, and what this would cost in taxes. The insurgents were freely giving their time to the public service on which they were engaged; unfair to tax them to pay the misguided men who stood in their way.

The judges, whose chief was David Sewall, honored the request with a written reply, but it wasn't a satisfactory reply. They referred the grievances of the people, including the question of pay for the militia, to the General

Court, and refused to bind themselves on the main point at issue. They had come, they said, "to administer justice impartially to all persons, agreeable to the laws of the constitution and government voluntarily entered into and solemnly certified by the people of this commonwealth, and no reasonable person can desire or expect they should do anything inconsistent with the important duties of their body."

When the significance of this reply had been digested and disseminated, Shays had more difficulty in holding his followers to his own standards of soldierly conduct. There had been, to be sure, no business transacted so far by the court. What with the confusion, it had not succeeded in paneling a jury until five o'clock on September 26, too late to begin hearings. On Wednesday the grand jury was of no service, for so ominous was the insurgent temper that the jurymen had to stand guard on the courthouse steps.

Nothing actually happened, but it looked at every moment as if something would. Shays' men, fretting under the stress of inactivity, with nothing to show for their long march, were growing mutinous, making threats, talking of kidnapping the judges and holding them as hostages. By Wednesday evening they were milling about the courthouse shouting for action. Shepard put all his men under arms, and spirited the judges away under guard.

By daybreak Thursday morning the insurgents were astir again. In respectable houses roundabout, frightened women, who had kept their doors barred since Monday, heard them and shivered. And everyone agreed on one thing; it was the people themselves who urged the rush on the courthouse; Shays was doing his best to hold them back.

They never did make the charge, for the judges gave

in. There was no general on this court; true, they all looked it for a while, for Shepard had brought them guns from the arsenal and asked them to mount guard. But it was too much. At nine in the morning the judges laid down their arms, entered the courthouse, opened court, but only long enough to adjourn it without day as specified. They did more. Privately they decided against going on to their next session, which was to have been Berkshire. In that county, as they well knew, not even the militia would defend them; they begged to be excused.

Shepard and Shays parted on amicable terms. Court having adjourned, Shepard gave Shays' men the pleasure of holding the empty courthouse, while he retired to secure the arsenal. Then on a prearranged signal both parties dismissed. Neither commander had any rancor against the other; so far as circumstances had permitted, they had actually collaborated to preserve the peace.

Shays went back to Pelham and husked his corn, glad of the comforts of obscurity again. But such comforts were not for him, or even for his feckless young friend Henry McCullough.

CHAPTER VII

Dignity of Government

ᶜᵗ ought to do *something!* Ye ought to do it *immediately!* Ye are hostile to the state if ye do less than all ye can to save it."

Thus young Fisher Ames in a loud voice crying in the *Independent Chronicle* over the signature of Lucius Junius Brutus. The date was October 26. General Court had been in session a month. In both houses the painful situation in Massachusetts had been ardently debated, but for all the legislative accomplishment so far achieved the delegates might have stayed home. General Court was, in fact, suffering something of a prolonged attack of legislative schizophrenia.

Proceedings had opened on Wednesday, September 27, while the forces of General Shepard and Captain Shays faced each other across the green in Springfield. News of the trouble there had reached Bowdoin just in time for him to insert a reference to it in the address he made to a joint session of both houses on Thursday.

Even in this situation the scholarly Bowdoin had spoken without histrionics; most of his talk was as colorless as his thin face. He had begun factually and dryly, a kind of gubernatorial "yours of the last instance received and contents noted," and went on to a schoolmasterly

84

insistence on the necessity of keeping order in the class-room.

"What led to the unwarrantable and lawless proceedings of these insurgents will be a necessary matter for serious inquiry," he said. "Investigating the true causes . . . may point out the proper remedy for the future."

What sort of investigation had he in mind? Did he mean study of conditions justly protested by the people or something quite different? When he went on to say that "good people" had been "unhappily and incautiously" led to support "the destructive measures which artful and wicked men have for some time been pursuing," it sounded as if his chief interest were in punishment, not correction. It was not unknown that Bowdoin was the recipient of warnings ascribing the disorders to British perfidy and a part of a "deeper plan than the sensible part of the community are aware of." Bowdoin was peculiarly vulnerable to such suggestion; he had a British son-in-law, a fact that gave rise to such gossip that he had taken office in 1785 with a self-imposed loyalty oath "that I am not, have never been, and (so far as a man can affirm in regard to his future conduct) will never be under any foreign influence whatever."

Bowdoin, however, did not ignore the grievances. It was, he said, the province of Legislature to redress them; appealing to any other body was an "unconstitutional and dangerous tendency even when attempted in a peaceable manner." The preservation of order depended on the people themselves. Those who permitted the contrary, either by direct participation, by tacit approval, or by lacking the courage to co-operate with the sheriff, were inviting disaster. They would look in vain for help from other counties, for it couldn't be summoned in time. Their own county would be "in danger of all the evils that may arise from a suspension or prostitution of law and justice," and without execution the laws of the country would be "as baseless as the fabric of a vision."

It was now for Legislature to "vindicate the insulted dignity of government," declared the Governor, and left his rostrum. General Court repaired to its respective chambers, the House so divided on the points at issue as to suffer a paralysis of will. It was left to the Senate to provide the firm course. Its members would not rule out consideration of the grievances, but in their eyes order was government's first law as it was heaven's. They gave their best attention to the means of restoring order, to what were to be called the "coercive measures," and in their framing Sam Adams, champion of the people, took the lead.

2.

By now a stiffening of the spirit, a hardening of the will, had come to Sam Adams. He had taken the lead in appealing to the disaffected through the address of the people of Boston, and what had been the reception? Largely sheer impudence. The claim of the people of Greenwich that they were dealing with oppression exactly as he had taught them to deal with it was a studied insult. What possible similarity could there be between taking a stand against the British and against a constitution which they themselves had ratified and against a government of their own election?

In late years Sam had become highly conscious of what was implied by "dignity of government." A young republic, not yet accepted among the concourse of nations, regarded even by some of its friends as unfit for survival in a world where the normal mode of government was monarchy, must guard its dignity as circumspectly as a young maid her maidenhead. For such reasons Sam as an officer in the republic had become a stickler for the proprieties. Few but his wife, Betsy, were now privileged to call him Sam. So watchful had he become for the decorum of the Senate that a junior senator who had innocently relayed a message that it was the business of the doorman to deliver had been overwhelmed by the blasting that he got from the Honorable Samuel Adams. The startled young man had even been threatened with expulsion for forgetting the dignity of his office.

What was happening now surpassed his worst nightmares. A handful of irresponsible farmers was causing the sovereign state of Massachusetts to cut a ridiculous figure in the eyes of the world. Persuasion had been tried, had been rebuffed. It was time to handle the situation with Spartan sternness. Sam's mind in times of stress always reverted to Sparta or to the early Roman republic. His political philosophy, so far as he had one, was a romantic blend of classical tradition and his notion of the old Puritan theocracy of the Mathers. He hoped to live to see his beloved Boston become the Christian Sparta. It was not now visibly moving in that direction.

Sam settled to the thankless drudgery that had been his lot ever since he had left his labors as the chief Revolutionary propagandist to take on the routine of Continental Congress and after that the Massachusetts Senate. What was needed was legislation with teeth in it. Sam worked on two acts: suspension of habeas corpus and a riot act.

Inspiration for the one had come from Bristol County, which, in spite of its quelling by Judge-General David Cobb, still evinced mutinous impulses. An official had written that it was of no use to jail leaders of the disaffected, since, no matter how closely the place was guarded, means would be found to break jail and release the prisoners. Transfer of such prisoners out of the county to Boston was the obvious solution.

The Riot Act was the suggestion of Theodore Sedgwick, who had recently investigated a rumor that Berkshire mobs were preparing to attack the Supreme Judicial Court. That the judges had decided against holding court was known, but the mobs, suspecting a ruse, had come anyway. Running across Sedgwick, they had hustled him rudely, and the affronted dignitary had since then been writing to Boston of conditions in Berkshire, his opinion of the faithless Judge Whiting, who encouraged such disorders, his conviction that the proper remedy was a riot act.

Sedgwick got his Riot Act. Sam Adams had no difficulty in getting it past the Senate, and with it the suspension of habeas corpus. But inducing the House to pass such measures was another matter. Too many in the House were of the belief that the way to restore order was so to rectify grievances that there would be no excuse for disorder. But debating this problem was simpler than solving it. The House had so far done little but debate, and meantime the "coercive measures" were thrust aside, though Adams, with insistent patience, came again and again to the House to inquire.

The measures had not been passed up to the time of Fisher Ames's "Ye ought to do *something*," but among the people of the disturbed counties, anxiously watching the debates in General Court, their existence was known. Because the measures were contemplated, the people were driven to act; because the people acted, General Court was driven to act in its turn. A complex interplay of action and reaction was set up that presently became a vicious circle. Out of the logic of these events matured rebellion.

It was a rebellion that no responsible man wanted, but it came anyway.

Rebellion Begins 3.

It did not come at once, and on the surface October was not a dramatic month. Across the state from the pleasant gardens of Boston, still hardly more than an overgrown country town, to the swamps of Hampshire and the wild upland pastures of Berkshire, spread the revolutionary flame, but it was most manifest in the familiar fire of the goldenrod, the scarlet and honey of the sumac and maple, and the clean bright leaves of the poison ivy.

Masses of wild asters dimmed the flame with their smoky blue; hunters burned off underbrush in the forest and put the taste of wood smoke into the mountain air. The lads shook down the hickories. The busy, intelligent hogs, who deserved better of fate, were lured from their rooting in the oak mast to come in and be slaughtered. Even in Pelham and Greenwich, people were not too troubled about what was going on in Boston to come to a neighbor's cornhusking.

But if life went on as before, there was still the sense of undercurrent, and presently of the swelling of an ominous tide. Even on the surface from time to time appeared tokens of uncontrolled forces.

There was the Worcester County convention, which opened in Paxton just as General Court opened in Boston. Nothing very new came of it, but its existence was disturbing, as if the forty-one towns represented had more faith in extra-legal assembly than in their lawful representation in Boston. Worcester town, which hitherto had ignored the conventions, sent delegates this time; so did Bristol County. In the interest of maintaining liaison it sent Captain Phanuel Bishop of Rehoboth.

The convention produced nothing more alarming than another petition to General Court. An attempt was made to co-ordinate it with the substance of other county petitions. The principal plea of the chairman was that the people keep order while waiting on the action of General Court. They seemed to be disposed to obey.

Yet the disposition was not universal. There was the aimless milling of the mobs in Berkshire on October 2 when they visited Great Barrington and Lenox to make sure that no court was held in either place. On the night of October 10 several men were caught trying to remove the cannon from Dorchester Neck. They were men from Bristol County, determined this time to give David Cobb a chance to die as general rather than sit as judge; they had five teams of horses with them.

The cannon was saved for the government, but after such an alarm a committee of both houses, headed by Sam Adams, waited on Governor Bowdoin to ask him to alert Cobb to the danger threatening two Taunton courts, scheduled for October 24 and October 30 respectively. Cobb, the last judge in the state to need alerting, again defended the law, and presently the most conspicuous of the Bristol insurgents, the George Brock who had written under the name of "Attleborough," was indicted, arrested, and brought to Boston.

It was late in the month before the real scare came. The cause was a circular letter dated October 13, approximately the time when Hampshire County had learned that the Riot Act had been drawn up in Sam Adams's Senate. The letter had been sent to selectmen of towns of known insurgent sympathies in both Hampshire and Berkshire counties, and circulated with such discretion that it was October 20 when General Shepard heard of it; he managed to get a copy, and sent it express to Boston.

"Gentlemen: By information from the General Court they are determined to call all those who appeared to stop the court to condign punishment. Therefore I request you to assemble your men together, to see that they are all armed and equipped with sixty rounds, each man to be ready to turn out at a minute's warning. Likewise be properly organized with officers."

It was signed "Daniel Shays." His name, he later protested, had been put to it without his knowledge; but it was there.

Whatever the effect of the letter on its intended recipients, the effect on Legislature was dynamic. Armed with such evidence the Governor demanded and got action from the reluctant House. The Riot Act passed October 28, and two weeks later the suspension of habeas corpus. When General Court finally adjourned on November 18, the Governor was fully empowered to call out the militia in force as needed and to send it wherever its services were required. He was now equipped to deal with any degree of emergency, except for one odd oversight; no one had thought to provide him the wherewith to feed and pay the troops.

One other defensive precaution was taken in a curiously roundabout way. Secretary of War Knox, returning to Congress from his inspection of the Springfield arsenal, thought the situation grave and induced Congress to authorize a contingent of troops to be stationed in Springfield to protect the public against "Indian" uprisings. The transparent ruse actually took in some partisans of government, who irritably remarked that it was strange for Congress to be harking back to the Indians when other dangers were clear and present. Not deceived at all were the insurgents, who had indeed cast a wistful eye on the arsenal stores.

4.

Those members of General Court who believed in conciliation rather than coercion had not labored altogether in vain.

That fear might have impelled the attack on the Springfield court was tacitly recognized by the passage of the Indemnity Act. It provided remission of sins to anyone taking a prescribed oath of allegiance before January 1 and abstaining from any further acts of violence in the meantime.

That few people could find money to pay taxes was recognized in a measure allowing for "the more easy payment of the specie taxes previous to 1784." Backlogs of taxes could be paid in goods which included nearly everything produced in Massachusetts: provision of all kinds, cordwood, pearl ash, sole leather, nails, cloth; warehouses for their deposit were to be set up throughout the state under the charge of a commissary general.

Some adjustment was made on the debtors' law. A committee had been appointed to consider the demand that General Court be moved from Boston. The question of official salaries had been looked into, and the House had acted to cut Governor Bowdoin's salary of £1,100. (The Senate, claiming constitutional objections, immediately gave it back.) Even Sam Adams had been sufficiently impressed by the outcry against the civil courts to cast about for a substitute. Not that he found one.

The major accomplishment of the Legislature was an Address to the People, drawn up on the premise that much of the unrest was based on misinformation. Rumor, for instance, had grotesquely magnified official salaries. The Governor was popularly supposed to be getting £60,000 a year and others in proportion, living soft and lush in Boston while they bled the people white. Even people too sensible to credit such exaggerations had a misty idea of the nature of government and the structure and purport of taxation.

The address undertook to enlighten them. Government, it was demonstrated, was not at all expensive. Salaries were listed beside the higher rates paid for the same offices under British rule. Public and state debts were explained and analyzed.

If not all "grievances" had been redressed, went on the address, let the people remember that "however great the public burdens are, attempts have not been wanting on our part to alleviate them; no member in the community is exempt from these burdens; the members of the Legislature have their full share, and can it be thought that they would designedly impose burdens on themselves or omit anything that might tend to their relief?"

Some matters were grievances only to a minority — for instance, the meeting of the General Court in Boston. "And must the minor part therefore rise against the government? . . . Unless we submit to be controlled by the greater number, the Commonwealth must break in pieces."

It was a long address; twelve hundred copies were printed to be distributed to ministers and town clerks. Ministers were to read it on Thanksgiving after divine service; clerks were to read it at the next town meeting, calling a special one if need be.

There was no stipulation as to what comment should accompany the readings. Most ministers could be counted on to provide a suitable gloss, but not all. A few, accord-

ing to the *Massachusetts Centinel,* "believed in county
conventions, the father of paper money, the communion
of insurgents, the iniquity of taxes, the forgiveness of
debts and in confusion everlasting."

In town meeting men rose to denounce the inadequacy
of what purported to be relief. Why "ease" the taxes
previous to 1784 and ignore the oppressive levies since
then? Why an Indemnity Act at all? Insulting to offer
pardon to people who had acted by the light of their consciences, and still more insulting the phraseology of the
offer — "deluded persons from a pretence of redressing
public grievances . . . have committed outrages. . . ."

The debtors' law, without quoting Scripture, still provided that "from him that hath not shall be taken even
that which he hath not." As of old, "for want of estate
sufficient to satisfy, it shall and may be lawful . . . to
take the body of such debtor and him commit to the common jail of the county, there to remain until he shall pay."

Nothing had come of all their petitions and patience.
The Court of Common Pleas still stood, and behind it
debtors' prison. The only choice they saw before them was
submission and serfdom, or to go on as before, unintimi-
dated by the "coercive acts," doggedly closing the courts
before they could do harm.

There was one exception: Bristol County. There, a
Boston observer reported, the people, satisfied that General Court had done everything possible, had settled down
to the peaceful and profitable occupation of nail-making.
The observer painted an idyllic picture of their new-found
content and suggested the remedy for the disaffected everywhere: let them make nails.

The observer couldn't have got about very much. Most
of the county had settled down indeed, but only because,
thanks to the vigilance of General Cobb, there was little

else it could do. Resentments smoldered long in Bristol County; more than elsewhere there was retaliation against informers, application of tar and feathers, burning of barns.

And fiery little Rehoboth, nerved perhaps by its proximity to Rhode Island, remained unafraid to speak its mind. Having duly listened on Thanksgiving to General Court's address, it called special town meeting on Christmas to fire its delegate, Stephen Bullock, for failing to accomplish anything better than that. Specifically it denounced his vote for the Riot Act and the suspension of habeas corpus.

CHAPTER VIII

"*A Bloody Day with Poor Job*"

By the end of November the "coercive acts" had been put into operation, and the result was an uproar that made all previous demonstrations seem like polite murmurs of regret.

On the other hand, the Indemnity Act, which offered insurgents a chance to repent their impetuosity and clear their records, had no apparent effect at all. This gesture of conciliation had passed Legislature in mid-November, just before adjournment, had received none of the publicity attending the coercive measures, and, according to Shays, many people failed to hear of it in time to qualify under it. The act offered pardon only to those who took an oath of allegiance before January 1 and refrained from violence "in the meantime." What was violence and what period did "in the meantime" cover? Specifically, what was the status of those who, in response to Shays' circular letter of October 13, had been rounding up town stocks of powder?

Shays, for one, was sufficiently interested to inquire. He didn't risk direct approach to authority, but asked a friend whose legal judgment he trusted to canvass the situation for him. The report was discouraging; Shays and his kind were considered to have disqualified themselves even before passage of the act.

Other men, who saw nothing criminal in closing the courts, saw no occasion for repentance. Legislature had done nothing to curb the Court of Common Pleas, which they considered an instrument of oppression; it was a patriotic duty to continue to remedy this oversight. Wherever the court proposed to open, it must be closed. Among those determined to pursue this course were Adam Wheeler, who had already been indicted by the Supreme Judicial Court in Worcester County, and Job Shattuck, the self-appointed Voice of the People in Middlesex.

2.

Oddly enough, officials in Worcester anticipated no trouble on November 21, when the Court of Common Pleas was due to resume its work interrupted in early September, and had taken no defensive precautions. When the insurgents came in, not more than 160 of them, but compactly organized under Wheeler, Sheriff Greenleaf had no better defense than a piece of paper. It was, however, a potent paper, the text of the Riot Act. He read it to them.

Wheeler and his men listened unmoved. They would disperse, they agreed, but not until the judges did. Judge Ward went through the empty formality of opening court in a tavern and of leading the judicial procession as far as the line of bayonets lined up on the courthouse steps. This time he wearily forbore duplicating his former feat of oratory. What was the use? It was the sheriff who, having read the Riot Act, attempted dissuasion. The intruders were shouting something about the high rate of court fees; the sheriff shouted them down.

"If you think court costs are too high," he roared, "I'll

hang every one of you gentlemen with the greatest of pleasure without charge."

He couldn't manage even that defiance with dignity. While he spoke, someone came up from behind and stuck a sprig of hemlock in his hat. Even his friends laughed, and the insurgents boisterously cheered. Not they but the judges presently dismissed.

At least the Riot Act had been read, and a number of the insurgents placed beyond the mercies of the Indemnity Act, especially their leaders, Wheeler and a Princeton man whom the sheriff noted only as Mr. Gale. Judging by the trouble he was in shortly after, it was Abraham.

The next session of court west of Boston must obviously be defended. It was Middlesex Court, due to take place on November 28, not in Concord, but in Cambridge. The insurgents might be expected to give Cambridge a wide berth, not only because it was on Boston's doorstep, but because when the Supreme Judicial Court had sat there late in October, government had made an impressive display of its power. Some two thousand militia had been summoned in its defense, and Governor Bowdoin, standing on the courthouse steps, for he was no horseman, had solemnly reviewed them.

But the dignity of the November court could not be left to past impressiveness. Two measures were taken for its protection. Those same citizens who had tried to champion the Concord court in September industriously circulated the county, exacting promises from insurgent leaders that this time they would not march. And in case promises were broken, a company of forty horsemen, commanded by Oliver Prescott of Groton, came in the day before court to police the grounds.

One of those approached by the peacemakers had been that Groton man of stormy history, Job Shattuck. He too, or so it was said, had promised to remain quiet. But it was a promise too difficult for Job to keep. Perhaps he felt that the government side had invalidated the promise by bringing in the horsemen. In any case, though the party of insurgents that set out for court was led not by him but by his neighbor Oliver Parker, aided by the loud-mouthed pugilist Nathan Smith of Shirley, Job followed secretly. He was watching the road for reinforcements from the west; Adam Wheeler was said to be on the way with a party from Worcester County; even men from Bristol were expected.

These plans came to grief. The Bristol County men never started; the Worcester men set out, but never made the rendezvous. Some seventy Middlesex men got as far as Concord, waited there for a time in confusion of purpose, and hearing that the government, armed with warrants for the arrest of their leaders, was about to take the initiative, scattered to their homes again.

That the warrants were out was more than mere gossip. Even two of the Worcester County men, Adam Wheeler and Abraham Gale, were on the wanted list, and the government sent armed horsemen in pursuit, sixty from Middlesex, a hundred from Boston. Adam Wheeler had a narrow escape; the Shirley men, including Nathan Smith, succeeded in hiding. But by the morning of November 30 two of the Groton men had been seized, and the horsemen were hard on the trail of the man they most wanted, Job Shattuck.

At the Shattack home they found only women and children; to judge by later report, they got in the way of the searchers and came in for some rough handling. They would, however, tell nothing of the whereabouts of the fugitive. It was an outsider (later punished for his helpfulness by the destruction of his potash works) who directed the government party to Job's friend Samuel Gragg.

Here again there were only women and children, who would tell nothing, and got pushed about. It was the weather, won to the side of government ever since Judge Ward's invocation, that provided the clue. Snow had fallen during the night, and there were fresh tracks in it. The party followed the tracks and brought their man to a stand on the banks of the Nashua, and called on him to surrender.

Surrender? Not Job. He put up, as one commentator put it, a fight "worthy of a better man and a better cause." When one Sampson Read laid hands on him, Job lunged, grappled, and the two of them rolled together down the icy bank. Better for the government's reputation if they had been permitted to fight it out, but Job was fighting like a cornered panther. He was trying to pull his sword, when F. C. Varnum, hovering above the combatants watching his chance, fetched him a blow in the knee with his own broadsword. Not even a panther can fight against the agony of a severed cartilage; the fight was over.

It was the first government victory over a genuine fighting insurgent. The troops loaded their captive into a "slay" and drove him to Boston in high spirits. Job would have been glad of a bullet to bite on. In Boston his captors dumped him down in jail along with Oliver Parker and Benjamin Page. All were held incommunicado.

It was, however, a costly victory for government. The disaffected were aroused as they had never been aroused before, by the bloodiness of the capture, by the mystery of the fate of Job.

"Tremendous times in Deed," wrote Job's friend James Parker in his almanac. "A bloodey day with poor Job." That was one of the more moderate comments. Others heard and believed that women had been mutilated, the eyes of a child gouged by government bayonets, and Job himself hacked to death.

Later when it appeared that Job, though maimed, was still alive, rumor had it that he was being atrociously tortured in Boston jail. Boston papers were presently forced to make a disclaimer. Shattuck, they reported, had been taken to a room "warm and comfortable with a good fireplace and capable of free ventilation, a room usually appointed for debtors, and accommodated with glass windows, where he was provided with suitable lodging, fire, and a faithful nurse."

It was true — by then — but without the clamor of Job's friends he might have laid forever on straw without attendance, faithful or otherwise. It was December 4, and Shattuck had already been in jail four days, before the Governor's Council, taking warning from the uproar, asked Jailer Otis to "furnish a woman nurse to attend Job Shattuck, and to prepare for his comfort . . . a bedstead and proper bedding."

3.

"The seeds of war are now sown; two of our men are now bleeding. . . . I request you to let this letter be read and for you and every man to supply men and provision to relieve us with a reinforcement. . . . We are determined here to carry our point. Our cause is yours. Don't give yourself a rest and let us die here, for we are all brethren. . . ."

To this document Shays signed his name unequivocally and without later disavowal. For men like him the situation had become simple and urgent. The episode in Middlesex had acted as a catalyst upon the earlier confusion of loyalties. Decent men had been robbed of their liberty,

transported away from their friends and a jury of their
peers to a dungeon in Boston, and Job Shattuck was crippled for life. The central issue was clear at last. The
loyalty of one neighbor to another in time of common
distress, the spirit that had brought the insurgents together in the first place, was now intensified into the
old revolutionary comradeship of brothers-at-arms. The
moral obligation to go to the rescue of Shattuck was as
compelling as if he lay wounded under fire on a battle-
ground.

Moreover, as Shays implied, there was another point;
everyone involved in the prior commotions had his own
neck to save.

Shays was writing on December 2 from Worcester,
where he and his friends had called an extraordinary meeting. His preparations were also extraordinary. He had
found barracks for the billeting of men from a distance
until such time as their services were actively needed.
These were not in Worcester, but nearly twenty miles up
the line in Rutland. Built to house some of Burgoyne's
army after the surrender at Saratoga, they were still
standing, and now other veterans of Saratoga were finding them serviceable.

Shays and Wheeler had been going about rounding up
town stocks of ammunition. In Shrewsbury they had had
a setback, for though the town was overwhelmingly with
them, it was Artemas Ward's town and by his foresight
the stock had been safely hidden. All Shays and Wheeler
got was a lecture from General Ward on their sins. It
would have been an excellent opportunity, murmured an
observer, to take both of them.

Shays' proclamation had gone nearly everywhere in
Worcester, Hampshire, and Berkshire counties. Even
Delegate Moses Harvey of Montague, to the detriment

of his later professional career, had had a copy and had urged its merits upon his fellow citizens. Shays was said to be expecting at least five thousand men in response. What was he proposing to do with them?

Worcester Court was to meet on Tuesday, December 5, and naturally must be stopped. But stopping court this far west of Boston was by now purely routine; five thousand men were hardly needed for the purpose. The favorite theory was that Shays planned a march on Boston to rescue the captives. There was even talk that he proposed to seize the Bank of Boston to provide the wherewith for paying his men. After all, the militia got paid; why not the Regulators?

General Shepard, writing from his home in Westfield at the height of the disturbance, thought that Shays had even more far-reaching plans. What could he be after, he asked, "unless it be the subversion of the constitution and government at one bold stroke . . . and to erect a military government for the coercion of the state by setting up his own standard . . . to be supported by great numbers from all the states, and be able to declare himself dictator of the whole union?"

It was a large order to attribute to a man who was more modest than not, aware of his own limitations, and, as observers in Worcester noted, even now more given to perplexity than to fanatic conviction. At the head of the movement almost in spite of himself, Shays was not of the stuff of which dictators are made. Rufus King spoke more pertinently when he remarked that the danger lay not with the current leaders of the rebellion, but in the probability that less naïve leaders might be attracted to it if it were successful. He had heard that Baron von Steuben, rather bored with all the time on his hands now that the Revolution was over, was taking an interest.

But this insurgent rally was not to be a success.

Though men were marching to Worcester from the Berkshires; though the militia of little Rowe, just beneath the Vermont border, was legended to have set out with instructions from town meeting to inquire into the premises of the respective factions and take the side they deemed just, few of these arrived.

Nor did Shays get to Boston. He was defeated not by Bowdoin, not by the light horse, but by the New England climate. The latter, as was so often to be the case in Shays' career, came out wearing white, symbol of the government's side.

4.

"At all hazards," decided Governor and Council on December 3, the court was to do business in Worcester, under the protection of the militia. Almost simultaneously, however, General Jonathan Warner was shamefacedly reporting that his militia was not to be depended on. A secret instruction was relayed to the judges; if court could not be supported, let it adjourn by proclamation.

On Monday the militia was mustered, and 170 actually reported to duty. They paraded to the courthouse, where they were faced by a "mob" of about 200 insurgents; these had been coming in for some days, and the evening before, a detachment had come from Grafton to take possession. Militia and mob met each other eye to eye; they were friends and neighbors, and where was their quarrel? Onlookers thought the mob looked "a little panic-struck." But it was the militia that wavered; while the mob stood its ground, the militia marched away and quietly dismissed.

It was on that Monday evening that the nor'easter began. In Boston it drove a brig ashore at Point Shirley and drowned five, blew the tide over the piers and ruined stores of sugar and salt. In Boston, in Worcester, then everywhere the great snow came, fine and dry and harsh against the face, drifting the roads, burying farmhouses to the eaves, dividing friend from friend and foe from foe, cutting off Berkshire from Hampshire, Hampshire from Worcester.

By the time the snow blew in on Worcester, the insurgent forces were estimated at a thousand. They dug themselves in as best they could. They plodded about town, looking for billets, but, being refused, went quietly away. They were ragged and hungry, for in spite of orders to provision, many had come with no more than a biscuit in their pockets; nearly to a man they were penniless, and what few coppers they had went to buy a warming dram in the taverns. Yet they did not force themselves on households who wouldn't have them, and they didn't pillage. They conducted themselves like the self-respecting yeomen they were, and even their enemies, who wrote their story, admitted this.

They had some friends in Worcester. One man was observed giving a shivering insurgent money with instructions "to lay it out for the good of the whole and not for his own use," and immediately afterward snapped at an acquaintance for using the word "mob."

"What would you call them?"

"Men!"

During the night a rumor came that the light horse was on the road from Boston, and those who had found quarters left them to mount guard at the courthouse. They knew how. It was little colder here and they no more ill-clad than they had been at Valley Forge.

The snow fell and the gale howled all day Tuesday. There was, under the circumstances, no court to stop, and the insurgents melted away until there were only 350 left in town. Some went to friends in the vicinity. Some went to the Rutland barracks, and here, until the storm blew out, was Shays himself.

He was, they said in Worcester, sick of heart and bewildered. Even the great Washington had sometimes hardly known how to make shift without proper provision and matériel. How then with Shays, who was no Washington, and whose men had little to stay them but their spirit? Some said there were as many as 2,000 of them biding their time in the environs of Worcester.

"For God's sakes, have the matter settled peaceably!" a government man quoted Shays. "It is always against my inclination that I take this business, but I could not withstand their importunity."

By Wednesday the storm had lifted, but the roads remained nearly impassable. There was no breaking through from Berkshire, and even from the Springfield area Luke Day and his detachment of 100 could get no nearer than Leicester. But somehow Shays managed to get his 350 men down from Rutland and paraded them into Worcester, riding at the head his white horse. Eighty came in from Belchertown, and by afternoon the insurgent force again had grown to 1,000. But Shays, who had expected so much more, was bitterly disappointed. Whatever he had expected to do here, he had at least counted on a massive demonstration of solidarity. What he had was less than the gathering in Northampton in August. This was no army to march on Boston, which, however, was paying him the compliment of expecting him. It would have taken a god out of Valhalla and an army of arctic-bred Vikings to have got up the Post Road through the forty miles of drifted snow that lay between Worcester and Boston, yet Boston lived like a city besieged, its streets bristling with muskets, and sentries at every approach.

Direct action being out of the question, the insurgents settled down to paper work. Their most far-reaching — and incriminating — enterprise was the division of the three western counties into military districts and the appointing of officers to command them. Prominent among these leaders, who became known as the "Committee of Seventeen," were Shays for Pelham, Luke Day for West Springfield, Alpheus Colton for Longmeadow, Captain Joseph Hinds for Greenwich. It was the duty of each officer to ask those towns in his district whose sympathy could be counted on to raise companies for the regimental command.

Addresses to the people were drawn up, setting forth the reasons for the Worcester gathering. These summarized the familiar grievances and added to them a protest against the suspension of habeas corpus and against the Riot Act, especially in that the latter gave "unlimited power to sheriffs and constables who might be "wholly actuated from a principle of revenge, hatred, and envy." Correspondence was set in motion with the towns asking them to petition the Governor for the liberation of Shattuck and his fellows and for a proclamation of indemnity to everyone connected with the stopping of the courts.

But the masterpiece was a petition that the body itself drew up for Governor and Council, a poignant if somewhat disordered composition reflecting their several moods of terror, desperation, and defiance.

"Your petitioners are not of the wicked, dissolute and abandoned," it read. Their cause "is not confined to a factious few, but extends to towns and counties and almost every individual who derives his income from the labor of his hands . . . or from a farm." They were motivated not by British instigation, but by "those sufferings which disenabled them to provide for their wives and children and the discharge of honest debts."

They claimed that the suspension of habeas corpus had resulted in atrocities: "The eyes and breasts of women and children have been wounded . . . the houses of the innocent broken into, their limbs mangled, their friends conveyed to gaol in another county and now languishing, if alive, under their wounds." Had even British abuses been worse? The release of the prisoners on good behavior was demanded, a new and more generous indemnity act, and adjournment of all the courts in the three western counties until after the May election.

Their rags, their hunger, the bitter winds that blew across Worcester shaped the final paragraphs. They were not afraid, they said, of death, war, or "the injuries of hunger, cold, nakedness and the infamous name of rebel, as under all these disadvantages they once before engaged and through the blessing of God came off victorious.

"To that God they now appeal, conscious of the innocence of their intention . . . from a love of the people and horror of the thoughts of the cruelty and devastation of a civil war. For the prevention of so great an evil your petitioners humbly pray for the love, candor . . . of your excellency and honors in releasing our unfortunate and suffering friends."

Then there was nothing to do but go home again. New rumors that the light horse was coming kept some of them traveling in companies. It was in any case a wise precaution, for a second storm had followed the first, and bitter cold. William Hartley, going it alone to his home in Williamsburg, fell in the snow and was found next morning frozen to death.

CHAPTER IX

"*What Shall We Do to Be Saved?*"

For God's sakes, what is the cause of these commotions?"
Thus in unwonted vehemence a Virginia gentleman who
had once in Cambridge had the effrontery to instruct
Puritan stock on their duties of attending divine service
and refraining from cursing.

"Do they proceed from licentiousness, British influence
. . . or real grievances which admit of redress? If the
latter, why were they delayed until the public mind had
become so agitated?"

George Washington was fair. He recognized what
Boston seemed determined to ignore, that there could be
grievances capable of driving honest men to desperation.
He was in a position to know. His own finances were in
disorder, for though he was more creditor than debtor, he
was unable to collect his due in anything better than what
might have been so much stage money. Like any farmer in
Hampshire, he was behind in his taxes, though not so far
behind.

But if Washington was one with the insurgents in believing that grievances should be redressed, he was one
with Bowdoin and his advisers in believing that govern-

ment should govern. The news of the turbulence in Massachusetts was to him like "an alarm bell in the night," to
quote one of his colleagues in a later context. He was
stirred not only to anger but to anguish.

"Are we to have the goodly fabric that eight years
were spent in raising pulled down over our heads?" he
asked his friend General Benjamin Lincoln. And to Henry
Knox: "You talk, my dear sir, of employing influence to
appease the present tumults in Massachusetts. . . . Influence is not government. Let us have a government by
which our lives, liberty and property will be served, or let
us know the worst at once."

The news was spreading. The commotions in Massachusetts were already in America a *cause célèbre,* and
ships carrying American papers were beginning to touch
foreign shores. Among the Loyalist exiles in Britain the
response was an unseemly chortle. "America exhibits a
curious scene at this time, rebellion growing out of rebellion," the *Bath Chronicle* observed when it had had time
to digest accounts of the incoherent events in Worcester.
"Particularly in that seeding bed and hotbed of discontent, sedition, riot and rebellion, Massachusetts Bay,
where rebellion originates, breeds naturally, thrives and
grows to maturity in the shortest time possible. There the
doctrine of civil liberty, or every man his own government,
has erected its standard and rides triumphantly over her
embattled plains."

Jefferson in Paris, by nature sympathetic with farmers
and their problems, took a philosophic view. From the
first he thought the people "not entirely without excuse."
Later: "The way to prevent these irregular interpositions
of the people is to give them full information of their
affairs. . . . If once they become inattentive to public

affairs . . . Congress and assemblies, judges and conventions, shall all become wolves."

Still later he blessed the rebellion with an approval that would have staggered Daniel Shays. "I hold it that a little rebellion now and then is a good thing, and as necessary in the political world as storms in the physical. . . . It is a medicine necessary for the sound health of government. . . . God forbid that we should ever be twenty years without such a rebellion. . . . The tree of liberty must be refreshed from time to time with the blood of patriots and tyrants. It is its natural manure."

Thus spoke Jefferson from a safe distance and from the godlike plane of detachment possible to men not immediately concerned with the painful exigencies of government. Men on the spot could not share his detachment. Washington was already dismally aware that his plans for spending the rest of his life in comfortable obscurity as a country gentleman were certain to be interfered with. Until now he had responded to most efforts to draw him back into public life with a sometimes irascible refusal. He had given the best of his life to winning the war; it was for others, for men more skilled in the dubious arts of politics, to win the peace. He would not listen to suggestions that he shame the rebels, many of them his late subalterns, by undertaking a personal, admonitory tour of Massachusetts. He would not commit himself on an invitation to go to Philadelphia in May to preside over a convention called to revise the Articles of Confederation. The proposal had his blessing; he had already participated in a convention in Annapolis that had somewhat unexpectedly resulted in the recommendation for the far more important convention in Philadelphia. But he would not go; one thing would lead to another, as well he knew. If he said

A, he would find himself committed to B, and good-by to his dreams of retirement.

But shaken to the core by the unpleasant events in Massachusetts — Massachusetts of all states! — by the revelation of fatal weakness in the whole structure of Federal government, in his heart he already knew that what was required of him he would have to do. His temper grew short when he considered these matters.

Young Alexander Hamilton, who was not disposed to retire and was already meditating the means whereby the thirteen disparate, contentious states could be melded into a firmer association, was wondering what would be the outcome of the commotions if they were "headed by a Cæsar or a Cromwell." Sam Adams also had Cromwell on his mind, but with a difference. Cromwell was his hero; had Cromwell's revolution taken root in a permanently Puritan England, perhaps there would have been no need for Americans to rebel. Now it was hard to play the stoic against the bitter knowledge that revolutions are not necessarily definitive, that so great a work as Cromwell's had been undone by the Restoration and King Charles.

In Massachusetts there was much talk of restoration, and not by Tories only. Representative government was demonstrably a fallacy, it was being said; the people were not fit to rule themselves. There was a craving for the comfort of a king, whose succession would be determined by God and not by an unruly, hare-brained electorate. Sam Adams could accept mockery and neglect for himself, but not for his life work. He shared the anguish of Washington, and, unlike Washington, he hardened his heart against the pretensions of this new, inglorious order of rebels who had dared steal the tools he had devised for a sacred cause and employ them in infamy.

Even the humorists couldn't lampoon the situation with

lightness of heart. What were called the Hartford wits were doing their best in *The Anarchiad*, modeled — as almost anything that rhymed was modeled in those days — on Pope.

There Chaos, Anarch old, asserts his sway,
And mobs in myriads blacken all the way;
See Day's stern front, behold the martial frame
Of Shays' and Shattuck's mob-compelling name. . . .
Thy constitution, Chaos, is restored,
Law sinks before thy uncreating word,
Thy hand unbars th'unfathomed gulph of fate
And deep in darkness' whelms the newborn state.

The *Connecticut Magazine* invited Massachusetts journals to copy these line and others; they were so copied, and read not always with laughter.

2.

If this was revolution, who was its Cromwell?

Authority already had a sizable list of minor Cromwells, for most of whom Governor Bowdoin had by now issued warrants for arrest. There was Job Shattuck of Middlesex, now placed out of harm's way by grace of God and Oliver Prescott's light horse. There were Adam Wheeler and the Gale brothers in Worcester County; Luke Day and his friend Elijah Day, and the ramifications of the Hinds family in Hampshire.

Something was being learned of the more active subversives in Berkshire. There was a Negro among them, a thirty-one-year-old Moses Sash of Worthington, who had been a private in the Revolution, but was a captain under Shays. Farmers near Bernardston were being rallied by Jason Parmenter and his sons and sons-in-law. In the region about Adams, insurgents were following the lead of

Eli Parsons, a veteran who had been wounded in 1777 and had endured with Washington the winter at Valley Forge. Parsons bore all the earmarks of a dangerous character and could express himself with more fire than Shays.

Then there was Shays himself. Certainly he was a figure to be reckoned with. He had been the leader in the gathering in Worcester in early December, and although this had been a fiasco from the insurgent point of view, it had been, under the circumstances, impressive, and was proof of a state-wide organization. For some time after, a force estimated at as many as five hundred had been kept together at the barracks at Rutland, and liaison had been maintained from Rutland with Berkshire, Hampshire, and Worcester counties. Given favorable conditions, a large force could be quickly assembled. This was revolution, and Shays was its Cromwell.

Yet many reports testified to an undictatorial diffidence on the part of Shays. Some authorities suspected that he was only a figurehead, that the strategy of the movement was being masterminded by a sinister power still unidentified. Probably the power was British; the Peace of Paris was still so recent that anything unpleasant that happened in America was bound to be ascribed to British perfidy. Through Shays, British George was obviously conspiring to get his colonies back.

Others, discounting such suspicions, accepting the movement at face value, thought that the real danger was that if successful it might attract a more skilled leader of unscrupulous ambition. This theory was supported by rumors that Shays was in fact trying to secure a more able command for his army. Reportedly he had approached Josiah Whitney of Harvard, who had come out of the Revolution a full colonel, and subsequently had become a brigadier general in the Massachusetts militia. Whitney

was outspokenly sympathetic with the insurgents; thanks
to him, the town of Harvard had voted against sending
its militia against them. But Whitney would not commit
himself to the extent of accepting a command.

Then Shays was believed to have offered the command
to none less than Colonel Ethan Allen of Vermont. There
was a proper Cromwell, or at least an inimitable Allen,
proper or not. But whatever Allen's inclinations, his state,
still unrecognized, still assailed by the territorial claims
of New York and New Hampshire, was in too delicate a
predicament for so prominent a citizen to risk antagoniz-
ing so powerful a neighbor as Massachusetts. Allen rejected the offer "with abhorrence," according to his
brother Ira. The abhorrence, some say, was merely for
the record.

3.

One of Governor Bowdoin's handicaps had been the
failure of General Court to provide funds to enable the
militia to take the field in force against the insurgents. In
Boston and Salem it was proposed to raise a fund by
private subscription to lend the state for this purpose,
and the loan was actively pushed early in December when
it looked as if an insurgent army might actually march on
Boston.

But the great doings in Worcester were snowed under,
the march on Boston petered out into a mere petition
which had miscarried, and the martial spirits of those who
were expected to put up the money also petered out in the
calm that followed. It wasn't until late in the month, a day
after Christmas, that an event occurred that frightened
Boston into putting up its money. Shays had stopped another court in Springfield.

There had been no prior intimation of just this event.

True, General Shepard had been fretting about his inability to keep his men together "especially in this season, without a daily allowance of spiritous liquors," with which he was inadequately supplied. Also he worried because Luke Day was drilling his men in West Springfield and Eli Parsons was reported en route with a provision train from the Berkshires.

But Shepard was by nature a worrier, and no one else seemed to share his apprehensions, certainly not the sheriff, who up to the very moment that the insurgents marched into town supposed that they had no designs on this court and accordingly collected no guard. Shays indeed was said to be out of the state, engaged in investigating the possibility of an alliance with Windham County, Connecticut.

But an hour before court was scheduled to start, in came the insurgents, three hundred of them, well armed, and at their head Luke Day, Thomas Grover of Montague, and Shays himself. The leaders carried a paper, drawn up the day before, and presented it to the judges: "We request the honorable judges of this court not to open said court at this time nor do any kind of business whatever but all kind of business to remain as though no court had been appointed."

The judges obliged. They too wrote a paper: "The justices of the Court of Common Pleas and the Court of General Sessions of the Peace now assembled at Springfield, in consideration of the opposition made to the opening of the said courts, have determined not to do any business or open the said courts at this term. Eleazur Porter, on behalf of said courts."

Nothing, barring the presence of the firelocks, could have been more orderly or more amicable. No one got hurt, no one so much as offered an insult. Two of the judges so entered into the spirit of the occasion as to sit down to dinner with Day and Grover.

Shays did not join them. He had dismissed his men, assuring them that he "was in hopes that he should not find it necessary to call them out any more on the like occasion." But he did not, according to Levi Shepard, Northampton apothecary, share the imperious exaltation of his two colleagues. "Shays is very thoughtful and appears like a man crowded with embarrassments."

Samuel Lyman, an aide to Shepard, detected signs of dejection in all three leaders: "They were under fearful apprehension of being taken and lodged with their friends Shattuck, Parker and Page." Lyman added philosophically that the "confused and confounded condition" of Massachusetts was characteristic of the whole union. "We do not yet feel that sameness or unity of interest which is the only cement for any nation — but this is not surprising, for our national existence is but of yesterday."

4.

Not two weeks after Springfield, Shays, going it alone down the road near his home in Pelham, found himself looking with difficulty into the eyes of his old commanding officer. With difficulty, not because he was ashamed, though he may have been, but because it had always been difficult to meet the eyes of General Rufus Putnam, who had a squint.

Shays had no reason to flinch from the encounter, though he knew Putnam's sentiments were not his own. The general made his home in Rutland, had once considered buying one of the barracks, of which Shays made intermittent use, to convert it into an academy. During the commotions they had sometimes met, and this would not be the first time the older man had reproved his former subaltern. It was reproof only, for Putnam, no longer in authority, had recently organized the Ohio Valley Company and was marking time until he could lead a band of settlers west.

During the war they had known each other well and affectionately, and Putnam was Shays' kind of general. Though his family was of older establishment in the country than George Washington's (like his second cousin Israel Putnam, he was descended from the Salem Village Putnams of witchcraft fame), he had been born to poverty. He had been reared by an illiterate stepfather who mocked the boy's attempts to "go as far in Arethmatic as to work the rule of three." Though Putnam had persevered, had grown into a man whose letters to Washington received warm answers, to this day his spelling was sometimes so outlandish as to require decoding; "proverbelly," he would write, meaning, as Washington would eventually deduce from context, "probably." Even Shays was handier with a pen than his general, though he didn't use it with such dogged persistence, or achieve under stress a similar rugged eloquence.

Their military experience had something in common. During the French and Indian wars Putnam had become an orderly sergeant, a status which he found "a good school for improvement," and, aspiring higher, he had diligently enlisted recruits for a company of his own, only to be cheated by one Captain Page, who "of all his father's children loved himself the best." He would not have been one to contemn Shays' similar efforts in 1777, or his pertinacity in hounding the authorities at West Point until he finally got his due. Putnam, of course, had risen higher. His absorption in "Arethmatic," and the providential circumstance ("infidels may laugh if they please") that just when he needed a plan to drive the British out of

Boston he found it in Muller's *Field Engineer,* which he managed to borrow from the reluctant General William Heath, had made a colonel and then a general of him.

But he had remained rough and burly in his ways. An observer from Pennsylvania had been scandalized to see him strolling through camp munching on a piece of meat he carried in his hand. He was accessible, an old friend, and Shays greeted him and eagerly asked him about what was uppermost in his mind.

What, he demanded, had happened to that petition sent from Worcester? That odd document, with its emotional logic, had seemed most admirable and persuasive to its framers. They had been waiting, as they reported when because of Putnam's answer they sent a second copy, "elated with high hopes of a kind reception . . . and gracious answer."

Putnam had heard nothing of it, but what, he asked, could they expect? "Since you and your party have once spurned at general mercy, it is absurd to expect that another general pardon will be granted."

"No? Then we must fight it out!"

Impossible, said Putnam. "You must either run [from] your country or hang, unless you are fortunate enough to bleed."

"By God, I'll never run my country!"

"Why not? It's more honorable than to fight in a bad cause and be the means of involving your country into a civil war. . . . You owned to me . . . that it was wrong in the people ever to take up arms as they did."

"So I did, and so I say now, and I told you then and I tell you now that the sole motive with me in taking the command at Springfield" — Shays was referring to the Superior Court in September — "was to prevent the shedding of blood, which would absolutely have been the case if I had not; and I am so far from considering it a crime that I look upon it that the government are indebted to me for what I did then."

Why then, asked Putnam, didn't he stop? The look of dread that others had noticed came over Shays' face. "It was noised about that the warrants were out after me, and I was determined not to be taken." But he denied that he had any hand in the order to collect men and supplies in Hampshire County; others had put his name to it. "I never had half so much to do with the matter as you think for, and the people did not know of the act of indemnity before they collected."

"But why didn't you take the benefit of the act as soon as it was published?"

It was a hard question. The circumstance that more than any other made the commotions look like full rebellion was the nearly universal failure of the rebels to take advantage of the Indemnity Act. Shays' reply indicated that the offer had caused serious discussion among the leaders, but that an authority had given "it as his opinion that the act would not have taken us in."

General Court might well have extended it to them nevertheless, said Putnam, and asked why Shays hadn't so petitioned before adding the crime of stopping Worcester Court to his score.

"It would have been better," admitted Shays, "but I cannot see why stopping that court is such a crime that if I might have been pardoned before I should be exempted now."

"When mercy has once been refused and the crime repeated, the government never can with any kind of honor and safety to the community pass it over without hanging somebody," explained Putnam. "And as you are at the head . . . I cannot see you have any chance to escape."

"I at their head! I am not!"

What then, asked Putnam, about his part in stopping the recent court in Springfield, and his signature on the paper handed the judges?

His name had been put to the paper without his knowledge, protested Shays. "I wa'n't got into Springfield when it was done. I told them it was inconsistent after we had agreed to petition as we did in Worcester, and promised to remain quiet and not meddle with the courts any more."

Putnam studied him thoughtfully.

"I'll ask you one question more. You may answer it or not as you please. It is this: had you an opportunity, would you accept of a pardon and leave these people to themselves?"

"Yes, in a moment!"

"Then I advise you to set off this night to Boston and throw yourself upon the mercy and under the protection of government."

"No, that is too great a risk."

"If your submission is refused, I venture to be hanged in your room."

But hanging was a matter on which Shays couldn't take a joke. "In the first place I don't want you to be hanged!" he snapped, and then ruefully: "and in the next place they wouldn't accept it of you."

The talk had consequences. Both returned to make arrangements to reach the Governor. Putnam labored to write a report, reproducing as faithfully as could be managed all the details of his talk with Shays; the latter ordered that a second copy of the Worcester petition be sent to Boston. In spite of his impetuous, unheroic exclamation, Shays made no effort to conclude a separate peace. But he did act on Putnam's remark that continuing to stop courts by force while waiting on an answer to the petition was inconsistent. Arrangements to stop a court in Worcester on January 23 were canceled.

It was not merely loyalty to Shays' orders that caused Worcester County insurgents to comply. The government had by now taken such action that they could hardly do otherwise. With sinking heart they saw the hated court open and take up again the sorry business of unforgiven debts.

"What shall we do?" observers heard them asking each other. "What shall we do to be saved?"

CHAPTER X

The Springfield Arsenal

When Putnam's account of his talk with Shays reached Governor Bowdoin, he was so impressed as to call an immediate meeting of his Council to discuss its implications. This was on January 17, eight days after the interview. Already, thanks to the energies of General Lincoln, an army was being raised to take the field against the insurgents. But the new evidence suggested that a peaceful solution was still possible, especially the report that Shays would accept a pardon even at the cost of abandoning his followers.

Why not put him to the test? Whatever the dark forces behind the rebellion — and even Shepard, who had at first thought it spontaneous, now believed the British were behind it — "the noted Shays" was the most conspicuous of its leaders; it was to his standard that the farmers rallied. In spite of his public appearances at Worcester and Springfield, he was elusive, not to be taken as easily as Job Shattuck. Besides, how much more disastrous to his cause if he were not taken by force but induced to surrender voluntarily.

Accordingly, a pardon was offered Shays on the condition that he leave his men, come to Boston, and promise to keep the peace. It was a certified offer; if after such compliance he were to be convicted by any court, he could count on full and free pardon by Governor and Council.

So much for Shays. There were also petitions from the people to consider. The one drafted in Worcester during the snows of early December had come at last, and with it a more recent document from Worcester County promising that the insurgents would not march against the court of January 23 if government forces were not sent to protect it. Both were shrugged off as improper and "absurd."

Petitions from sundry towns were held over for the consideration of the General Court in February. Typical was one drawn up by Gardner town meeting on January 15. It urged Governor and Council to do everything possible to restore peace, "even the liberating of Captain Shattuck and others who are confined in any of the gaols of the Commonwealth . . . if it could be without a trial, if not, that they may have it as quick as may be, and even if found guilty they may have a pardon; and that no more of that party be taken if there is any likelihood of there being any means of settling the matter." Gardner pleaded also for suspension of the courts: "We had better suffer a little than a civil war should take place."

The effect of such petitions was weakened by evidence that not all of them represented unanimity of sentiment in the towns involved. One dated December 7 from "a committee of the body of Holden" — both date and term were suspect — had been followed by protests from the contrary-minded of Holden, one signed by eleven citizens, one by thirty. The former said that they would not ask what government could not grant, and in the case of the prisoners: "we cannot conceive that we ought to interfere, as they have acted with their eyes open after the government had pardoned a first offense." A lone Holden man,

one Isaiah Brown, said of the authors of the first petition
that "they are as deep in the mire as they are in the dirt."

Yet even at this date and confronted with this evidence,
Governor and Council were prepared to pardon the greatest rogue of them all if he came in and asked for it. Implications might be read into the offer to Shays, the possibility that other leaders might hope for mercy if they
repented in time. It was a last chance for redemption;
under the terms of the Indemnity Act, the bulk of the
insurgents had already disqualified themselves for pardon.
Almost the only insurgents who had take the oath of
allegiance were the prisoners in the Boston jail. Job Shattuck had taken it late in December when even his fighting
spirit recognized that he was done for.

Government, however, had shown no inclination to
pardon these penitents. It was under no obligation to do
so, since they had disqualified themselves by acting after
publication of the Indemnity Act. But other insurgents,
confused and frightened and imperfectly acquainted with
legal technicalities, could see in the circumstance only one
point — that mercy had been asked and had not been
granted.

Shays himself to the end of his days may never have
known how close he had come to pardon. Putnam, entrusted to deliver the offer, saw Shays again, but under
such circumstances that pardon could no longer be dis-
cussed. The relentless pressure of events had forced both
sides into a position from which neither could retreat, and
Putnam returned the Governor's offer to Boston, lest it
fall into the wrong hands.

2.

The first half of January 1787 was on the surface so
peaceful that people of easy optimism assumed that the

trouble was over. Under the surface, however, events were shaping to a tragic climax.

An army was being raised in the eastern half of the state. Shays' second invasion of Springfield had at last stung the property-holders of Boston into putting up their money. General Benjamin Lincoln, appointed to command the government forces when funds could be raised to equip and pay them, had been going about the coffee houses and laying the situation and the proposition in plain language before the merchants he found there. A total of £5021/18 had been raised — at least on paper — during the first week in January in subscriptions ranging from £30 to £300, a few to be paid in provision but most in cash. Governor Bowdoin headed the list with £250. Since the estimated cost in specie of keeping five thousand men in the field for thirty days was £6,000, this was better than a beginning.

Lest the details of these martial preparations escape the attention of the insurgents, Governor Bowdoin made their purpose clear in an address to the people on January 12, in which he announced his intention to call on his full powers to call out the militia of the several counties to protect the court at Worcester.

"It is now become apparent that the object of the insurgents is to annihilate our present happy constitution," he said. Their success would be "the result of force undirected by any moral principle; it must finally terminate in despotism — despotism in the worst of its forms. Is the goodly fabric of freedom which cost us so much blood and treasure so soon to be thrown into ruin? Is it to stand but just long enough to flatter the tyrants of the earth in their daring maxim that *mankind is not born to be free?*"

For a month already efforts had been made to enlist volunteers in the government forces. Just as a happier, younger Shays had in 1777 sought to better his rank by enlisting a company from Hampshire County, young Ensign John Pyncheon of Salem was hustling about Essex County, beating up recruits, lodging them in bad weather in his own home, escorting them to Boston, rejoicing or repining as they passed muster or were rejected, hoping for a captaincy.

On Thursday, January 18, he was ordered to lead a company to Woburn; and his father, though of frank Tory sentiments, one whose windows had sometimes got smashed during the Revolution, and theoretically one of those who should have abetted the present turbulence, found his sympathies suddenly all with the efforts of the new government to put down a newer rebellion.

3.

These preparations in the east had not gone unmarked in the west. Though there were no current disorders, the insurgent communities were seething with activity born of panic. On the one hand, men were mustering to defend themselves against Lincoln's army; on the other, men from several communities, not unsympathetic with insurgent aims but appalled at the prospect of bloodshed, were imploring both sides to desist.

The response to the Governor's proclamation had been an order from five insurgent leaders, among them Shays, commanding the district officers to assemble with ten days' provision at Pelham by Friday, January 19. The government, read this statement, was determined to support the courts "by the point of the sword . . . to crush the power of the people at one bold stroke and render them incapable of ever opposing the cruel power of tyranny, by bringing those who stepped forth to ward off the evil that threatens the people . . . to an unconditional submission and their leaders to infamous punishment."

Thanks to the efforts of Shays in Pelham and of Lincoln in Boston, by January 19 the state was forming into two armed camps. The militia had been called out to the number of 4,400 and was mustering in Boston, Worcester, and Springfield. Volunteer units, like that commanded by Ensign Pyncheon, were setting out in high spirits. It was 1775 all over again, commented Bostonians, reconciled at last in all this joyous bustle to the necessity of using force.

In the western part of the state there was a similar stir, but with little lightness of heart. It was no longer a matter of riding to town to stop court, but of defending themselves against a force superior in numbers and immeasurably superior in arms. If their case was desperate, the alternative, the gallows, was worse. In Worcester County, throughout the Connecticut Valley, and the Berkshires, farmers were throwing down their winter chores and mustering against the foe. By January 20, Shepard at Springfield heard that Luke Day had four hundred in West Springfield, that six hundred were expected under Eli Parsons from Berkshire, that Shays was collecting his forces in Pelham and Greenwich. They were men who knew their business, for, barring boys, they were largely veterans of the Continental Army.

Their object was plain: the Federal arsenal with its barracks, its stores, its field pieces. They were somewhat better armed than they had been before, thanks to their possession of such town stocks as they had been able to lay their hands on, but they were by no means well enough equipped to hope to stand against a force like Lincoln's. Shepard needed no agents to inform him that their only hope lay in occupying the arsenal and turning its artillery on Lincoln when he came.

To stand them off, Shepard had only nine hundred men,

including militia units of variable loyalty. And General Lincoln with his army was still several days away.

Yet even in insurgent country there were men daring enough to try to avert a fatal collision between the opposed forces. Three towns in Worcester County — Worcester itself, Sutton, and Holden — sent committees to reason with both the insurgents and the Governor.

In Adam Wheeler's Hubbardston they had some initial success with Henry Gale. Though he had flung himself into the insurgent movement while Shays was still hesitating, like Shays he was a man of divided heart. He had once considered taking his oath under the Indemnity Act, but had been "afraid the light horse would take him and abuse him as they had Captain Shattuck." Now at first he promised the mediators he would sign any paper, take any oath unconditionally. "For God's sakes, don't leave us until something is done!" begged Gale.

But Adam Wheeler and his colleagues looked at Gale's soul-searching grimly. "There are enough of us to take care of him," one of them said. And another: "If we don't all git together, we'll be taken." Gale, "sick of the job" though he was, remained with Wheeler.

In the meantime, Amos Singletary, Sutton representative to General Court, was in Boston. Old "Daddy" Singletary, self-educated, a Bible-thumping churchman ever since he had married him a pious wife, was famous for his salty contributions to public debates from as far back as the Provincial Congress. Governor Bowdoin could not deny him audience, and listened gravely to Singletary's plea that Lincoln be restrained from marching to Worcester. The people themselves had promised not to interfere with court, said Singletary; their word could be counted on. The presence of the government troops could have only bad consequences.

But Bowdoin shook his head. Singletary had come too late. It was already January 21, and at dawn the day before, Lincoln had set out. The government had committed itself to force and there was no recall.

4.

With heavy heart General Shepard watched Shays drawn near the arsenal. This was no parade; Shays marched his men up the Post Road in open column by platoons. There seemed to be at least twelve hundred of them. This time they were not to be appeased by an empty concession, like letting them occupy the courthouse.

It was nearly four o'clock in the afternoon, January 25, a fine cold day with crust on the snow. Shepard was aware of the crust because it had cut the legs of the horse of Deputy Sheriff Abel King, who had ridden across lots from Wilbraham the day before to bring intelligence of Shays' plans.

In some ways Shepard knew more about those plans than Shays did. Shays had sent to Luke Day at West Springfield commanding a junction of their forces for their attack on the arsenal. Day had replied that he was unready; he would make the rendezvous at the same hour on the twenty-sixth.

Why unready? Some said that Day's vanity demanded a more decisive voice in Shays' councils; after all, he had been in rebellion the longer time; it might as well have been named Day's Rebellion as Shays'. Others said that Day was also of divided mind. He had been in consultation with his pastor, Dr. Lathrop, whose favorite text was "if ye refuse and rebel, ye shall be devoured by the sword," and had been left shaken by the interview.

Whatever his reasons, it was Shepard, not Shays, who

had the reply, intercepted at a tavern. Shepard, not Shays, knew that the attack would be unsupported.

But Shays was in no position to wait. Lincoln had reached Worcester and was pressing on in spite of the cold and a message from Shays promising to send his men home if an amnesty could be granted until a new session of Legislature could act on the complaint of the insurgents. Lincoln had no faith in the promise and was marching his forces up the Post Road. If Shays were to take the arsenal, it was now or never.

Shepard had been in contact with Shays through his aide Samuel Buffington, who, going down the road toward Wilbraham to reconnoiter, had earlier run across Shays' army at a halt five miles out of Springfield. There he met an insurgent officer, who referred to Shays as general, and said: "If the matter isn't settled by sunset, New England will see such a day as she never has seen yet."

Shays himself came up, with drawn sword in one hand and a pistol in the other. In action, at the head of his troops, he was a different man from the doubter Putnam had talked to on a lonely road. Nevertheless, Buffington undertook to read him a sermon.

"I'm here in defense of that country you are endeavoring to destroy," he began it.

"If you are in defense of the country, we are both defending the same cause," retorted Shays.

"I expect we'll take different parts before night."

"The part I'll take," said Shays, making a small joke, "is the hill on which the arsenal and the public buildings stand. . . . Will they fight?"

"You can count on it."

"That's all I want!"

"If you advance," said Buffington, "you will meet those men we are both accustomed to obey."

Men who were accustomed to obey; men who have loyally served. Shepard, watching the advance of Shays, whom he knew to be "a brave and good soldier," picking out the faces of others with whom he had served during the Revolution, wondered how it would be possible to give the order to fire. If he must, he would give it, but would it be obeyed? His men, like him, were spotting old friends.

They saw grizzled Jason Parmenter; they saw Daniel Luddington of Southampton, James White of Colrain, Alpheus Colton of Longmeadow, the latter a young laborer in his twenties.

Would the men at the arsenal actually fire on their friends and neighbors? How had Joseph Hawley of Northampton put it? "Were they the common enemy we could bear it, but they are our equals, our acquaintances, our brethren. . . . Impossible for us to defend ourselves against our brethren because we cannot fight them."

But the same held for the other side. When it came to a point, could Shays' men be induced to fire into the faces they too were picking out? Could Shays himself give such an order? What did the man want? Shepard sent Buffington to ask him. "Barracks and stores," said Shays.

At 250 yards from the arsenal he made a halt and gave Shepard a second chance to send aides to him, warning that he would be fired on if he drew nearer.

"That's all we want!" stoutly replied Adam Wheeler, who took this message. Shays' army resumed its march, this time on the double.

At 100 yards Shepard ordered the artillery to open up. The first two shots were deliberately aimed above the heads of the men, and still they came. It was what they must have expected. Their brothers at the arsenal could not do otherwise when, in the words of a song still unwritten, their cause it was just.

But the third shot was aimed into their column, and at the fourth or fifth the movement was suddenly away from the arsenal, and nothing Shays could do could rally them.

"Murder!" they cried as they ran. "Murder!"

They left behind them three dead, Ezekiel Root and Ariel Webster of Gill, Jabez Spicer of Leyden; and one John Hunter of Shelburne was so badly wounded that he died later.

On the government side only one was wounded, and he, as Shepard put it, by "inattention." John Chaloner had stepped in front of his own piece of artillery just as it was going off, and lost both of his arms. That the insurgents had been armed was proved by three loaded muskets picked up with the dead. But they had not fired a shot. If Shays was a Cromwell, he was one still guiltless of his country's blood.

"Sir," Shepard wrote Governor Bowdoin next day when he had pulled himself together, "the unhappy time has come when we have been obliged to shed blood. . . . Had I been disposed to destroy them, I might have charged upon their rear and flanks with my infantry and two field pieces and could have killed the greater part of his whole army within twenty-five minutes."

But Shepard had been unable to bring himself to that; not a musket, he reported, had been fired on either side. Would they have fired if so ordered? It had been in its small way a pushbutton war. A howitzer, of which Shepard had one loaded with grapeshot, can be managed impersonally, can be discharged without too close inspection of the faces of the target.

CHAPTER XI

Degree of Innocence

♪♪

Bad news from camp today," James Parker of Shirley remarked in his diary two days after the clash in Springfield. And later: "News flying everywhere these days and the whole state in an uproar. Shays and General Lincoln and their men on the move back and forth. It seems as if the people ware mad as they really are. Strange times in Deed."

The nature of the news flying irresponsibly about was summarized by a correspondent of the *Massachusetts Centinel*. Shays at the head of 15,540 had returned fire on the arsenal, killed seventeen, captured all the Continental stores, and taken thirty-two prisoners, among them General Shepard. Ethan Allen was marching to Shays' assistance from Vermont with an army of ten thousand; a thousand were coming to him from three counties in the Province of Maine; seven hundred insurgents had mustered in Marblehead. General Sullivan of New Hampshire was hiring Lincoln's light horse at fifty dollars a head. The British fleet lay offshore, ready to take over when Shays completed the rout of the government forces.

Shays himself meanwhile, like any proper folk hero, chivalrously scorning mere numerical superiority (the fig-

134

ures in the rumors gave him 27,240 against General Lincoln's puny 5,000), had challenged Lincoln to decide the issue in single combat.

These reports from a Boston journal had a satiric edge. Possibly such yarns were credited thereabouts, but certainly not in Hampshire County, where the sorry truth was all too evident. Yet even Shepard was susceptible enough to the tenor of such talk to be nervously bracing himself for a second attack. However demoralizing for Shays' men the outcome of the first, their forces were intact, and now they had been blooded. If they came back they would be in a dangerous mood, and if they were joined by Day's company they might succeed.

For more than forty hours Shepard waited, and then at last he was relieved. At noon on January 27 another army came marching up the Post Road—Lincoln's. It had stopped in Worcester only long enough to protect the court and assist the sheriff in arresting some malefactors. One of these was no less than the Reverend Caleb Curtis of Charlton. Not only had he been urging his parishioners to follow Shays — "if we drop it now, we lose all" — but he had invoked the Lord's aid before they set out; his very prayers were subversive.

After Worcester, Lincoln had moved his men up the road in forced marches.

He had with him four regiments, comprising both militia and volunteer companies, three companies of artillery, and his famous light horse. The men came from Essex, Suffolk, Worcester, and Middlesex counties, but the last two were not represented in full strength. The second regiment of Shattuck's Middlesex had assembled only to vote to stay home, with the blessing of their general, Josiah Whitney, and those who came were less than wholehearted. Arrived at Springfield, Lincoln presently dismissed what was left of the Middlesex militia without waiting to conclude his business with Shays.

Briskly Lincoln took over. He was a man of sanguine temper, immune to the melancholies that so often beset Shepard, who, living in rebel country, was subject to more powerful pressures than his superior. Lincoln, to be sure, had infirmities of his own. Wounded at Saratoga, one leg remained shorter than the other, a disability that he disguised by wearing specially constructed boots. He also had an embarrassing tendency to "somnolence." In the saddle, in council of war, in the act of dictating a dispatch, he would suddenly nod off. Then there was nothing his aides could do until, as suddenly rousing himself, he went on with the business in hand as vigorously in command of its details as if he hadn't dozed. A six-footer, he hardly looked his height, for he was nearly as broad as he was long.

Lincoln's troops were tired from the long march up icy roads, but he was not the man to let them rest. Before evening, when his whole army reached Springfield, he had already acted to head off the junction of Shays and Day. His men crossed the Connecticut on the ice, routed the guard at the ferry, and stampeded West Springfield. Insurgents and some townsmen took flight with such precipitation that Lincoln's men were pleased to find good insurgent pork and beans still baking in the ovens.

They were not, however, given time to enjoy the beans. Under Buffington the cavalry was dispatched right up the Connnecticut ice to head off Day from crossing to the east bank. Others followed Day overland in the direction of Southampton and Northampton, picking up discarded equipment as they went. On the east bank a force headed by Shepard went after Shays himself, who since his repulse had been encamped at Chicopee.

2.

From Chicopee, where he had joined forces with Eli Parsons, Shays had sent back a message to Shepard: "Sir, I desire you to send my dead and wounded by my flagg, so that I can burye my dead and take care of my wounded." Legend has it that Shays overestimated the number of his dead and that Shepard, snapping out of the unprofessional pity that had nearly mastered him at the time of the attack, retorted that he lacked so many corpses "but that if Shays would attack the Arsenal again General Shepard would furnish him with as many [dead] rebels as he should desire."

From Chicopee, Shays fell back to South Hadley, his numbers somewhat diminished, for two hundred were reported to have deserted, if it can be called desertion when a hungry man goes home to a square meal. His forces still numbered over a thousand, and now it was plain that they were desperate men. Gone were the days when they would, as at Worcester, diffidently knock on the door to state their needs and take no for an answer. Their situation had gone beyond mere politeness. They had seen comrades die; forces superior to theirs and vastly better armed were on their heels. Everyone from Shays down had visions of the gallows. Whoever wasn't with them could take the consequences.

At Hadley there was an incident. An advance unit which had stopped to eat at Butt's tavern — they must have cleaned out the place, for there were said to have been five hundred of them — were fired on by government soldiers hidden in an outhouse. One man, Amos Call of Montague, mistaken in his Continental buff-and-blue for Shays himself, was killed and another injured.

Shays arrived and got the snipers to surrender by

threatening to burn the house down if they didn't. But after that no command by Shays could restrain his men from breaking, entering, and looting, especially those houses that had been abandoned by their owners. Two barrels of rum became their most prized booty.

Amherst, which his army reached by eight in the evening, was so loyally insurgent a town that when Lincoln followed a few days later he found hardly an able-bodied man in the place; they had all followed Shays.

The "Hamptons" on the other side of the river were a different story, as Day was finding in his parallel retreat through Southampton to Northampton. Captain Joseph Cook, jailkeeper, refused to give up the key to his jail even when he was dragged in his nightclothes out into the snow. In their search for the key the insurgents were outwitted by Mrs. Cook, who refused to leave bed and hid the key under its covers, or who dressed and thrust the key down her bosom, or perhaps hid it in the trundle bed of her children; the multiple choice by courtesy of local legend. All versions agree that the key was successfully defended and that keeper Cook died within the year as the result of his exposure in the snow.

On January 28 Shays fell back to Pelham. From farmhouses along the road from Amherst, women and children came out to stare at the march of more than a thousand armed men through the snow. The best of them were shivering, and most of them were famished. But there was cheer of a sort in Pelham. Ten sleighloads of provision managed to elude Lincoln to reach it. And in Pelham, Daniel Shays was at home.

Pelham had two hilltops. West Hill, the lower, commanded the approach from Amherst; Conkey's tavern was in this neighborhood. On the wind-swept summit of the higher East Hill stood, as they stand today, two white buildings, the little meetinghouse where Burroughs had once preached, and the town hall; in God's acre behind them was the cemetery.

Shays disposed his army between the hills, taking pains to keep the steep, circuitous roads well posted with sentinels. His officers he treated at Nehemiah Hinds's tavern on East Hill, for in Pelham his credit was good.

Here he made his headquarters for a few days, and at this point, as one observer irritably commented, activities were confined to letter-writing: Lincoln to Shays, Shays to Lincoln, Lincoln to Shays.

3.

Lincoln's force had stopped at Hadley. The little town on the east bank of the Connecticut had overnight become a garrison. Field pieces had been set up by the meetinghouse; the home of Sheriff Elisha Porter was the general's headquarters, and 3,100 men were billeted in the village. Every home and most likely every barn and outhouse had its quota.

Daily the troops mustered not only to drill but to hear prayers. These were said from a pulpit cut from a snowbank near the sheriff's house. The local preacher, Dr. Samuel Hopkins, undertook them at first, but his voice wouldn't carry; Dr. Joseph Lyman of Hatfield replaced him and uttered prayers "that could be heard distinctly by the entire army."

Shays was less than a dozen miles away, but his position even without field pieces commanded respect. He could hardly be dispossessed without slaughter, and for the latter, Lincoln had no more stomach than Shepard. The enemy was, after all, made up of homespun farm folk, as diligent as his own men in listening to prayers. Reasoning might still serve better than assault.

On January 29 he sent three officers, among them General Putnam, who had now attached himself to his staff, with a message to Shays pointing out that resistance was hopeless and asking him to avoid bloodshed by disbanding his "deluded followers." If they surrendered and took the oath of allegiance, Lincoln would recommend the privates "to the General Court for mercy. If you should either withhold this information from them or suffer your people to fire upon our approach, you must be answerable for all the ills which may exist in consequence thereof."

The mission, riding up the hills to Pelham, found Shays' forces on the alert. A sentinel challenged them with a rifle shot, but finding that they came "with a flag from the government army," admitted them to the quarters of "the celebrated Mr. Shays." The latter, always punctilious in matters of military courtesy, received them "with a considerable show of civility and politeness" and promised a reply as soon as he could consult his staff. The messengers themselves had a chance to chat with some of the latter, among them Adam Wheeler, and got the impression that "a general pardon is become the ultimate and only objective."

Did Putnam confide the fact that he still carried in his pocket an offer of full and free pardon for Shays himself? Putnam considered that Shays had forfeited such an offer and that evening returned the document to Boston. Yet he may have dropped some hint of what he had with him, for later he was privately and urgently approached.

Their "cause was just," Shays and his staff replied to Lincoln's delegation. They were confident that they had the majority of the people on their side, and would stay quietly in Pelham if Lincoln would remain in Hadley until General Court acted on their petition. The Legislature was in fact just assembling in Boston.

After the delegation left, Shays' staff labored over a more formal reply, couched in the dignified rhetoric compulsory on such occasions. They began by listing the counties from which their army was assembled: Middlesex, Worcester, Hampshire, Berkshire. "Taking into serious consideration the purport of the flag just received, return for answer," they wrote, "that however unjustifiable the means may be which the people have adopted in having recourse to arms, various circumstances have induced them thereto. . . . That virtue which truly characterizes the citizens of a republican government hath hitherto marked our paths with a degree of innocence." They were "unwilling to stain the land, which we in the late war, purchased at so dear a rate, with the blood of our brethren and neighbors." They would lay down their arms on two conditions: a general, not a limited, pardon; and Lincoln's army to cease hostilities and retire to Boston until the General Court could act on "our united prayers."

Thus the reply to Lincoln of Shays' general staff. It was accompanied by another document, signed by Francis Stone as chairman of the counties. Framed as a petition to the Legislature, it also acknowledged wrongdoing in taking up arms and expressed the hope of avoiding bloodshed. Without an early reconciliation, it warned, this might be impossible. Only on the promise of a general pardon would the men lay down their arms.

These replies were brought to Lincoln on January 30 under the protection of a flag of truce by Stone himself, Eli Parsons, and Sylvanus Billings. Sheriff Porter, who had a state warrant for Billings, took the opportunity to seize him as he was in the act of dismounting before Lincoln's headquarters. Lincoln was then faced with a difficult decision. Which took precedence, the flag or the warrant? He decided in favor of the more ancient emblem and with some difficulty persuaded the sheriff to let Billings go. Not all Hadley citizens appreciated the chivalric gesture.

Lincoln's reply to the petitions was curt. He had no authority to grant a general pardon and said so. When this reply reached Pelham no one felt safe.

One last appeal came down from the hills. On midmorning of Saturday, February 3, Adam Wheeler came to ask General Putnam that the pardons offered privates be extended to the officers. "I would throw myself on the mercy of government," said Wheeler, "if I weren't afraid of my own men, who . . . declare that they would murder any one of their leaders if they attempt to leave them or make any separate terms for themselves."

It was a somewhat graceless appeal of dubious veracity. One officer, Henry Gale, had left Pelham and his command and had gone home to throw himself on the mercy of government. He had not been detained and he had not been murdered.

No one, in any case, took Wheeler's plea too seriously. He was believed to be interested in gaining time. At noon, soon after the interview, scouts brought Lincoln word of a troop movement in the hills, at the time apparently only from West Hill to East Hill. Lincoln, suspecting more, kept his scouts on the watch. But it was long after sundown when he learned that Shays' army was in fact on the road, that they were leaving Pelham for Petersham, twenty miles to the northeast. One would have supposed, and certainly Shays did suppose, that he was safe from pursuit at an hour so late and in the dead of winter.

But Lincoln was hardy and eager for action. His orders went out at once. By eight in the evening his men, loaded with three days' provision, were on the march, setting out in the starless dark up the drifted hills through the bleakest country in Massachusetts east of the Berkshires.

4.

This time the weather was on the side of the insurgents. It had beguiled Lincoln into setting out by offering an evening of deceptive mildness. But at two in the morning of Sunday the fourth, when the bulk of Lincoln's men had passed the halfway mark at New Salem, it suddenly opened up on them with a bitter blast from the north. In the gale the temperature plummeted, freezing yesterday's new-fallen snow and driving it sharp as needles into their faces. Many supposed they were caught in a blizzard.

Blinded, gasping for breath in the wind, their feet, faces, and hands frostbitten, the men struggled on toward Petersham in a more brutal march than any could remember from the Revolution. There was no cover and nothing for them to do but keep moving. Lincoln's impetuous daring was about to present Shays with the opportunity of a lifetime. It was broad daylight before the forward units stumbled up the steep and narrow approach to Petersham. No tactical genius was needed to overwhelm them before their frozen hands could unlimber the field pieces they had dragged with them. Only a minimal alertness was necessary to crush the invaders.

Shays had his great chance — and he muffed it. The minimal alertness had somehow not been provided. His army too had had a hard march, though under better conditions than Lincoln's, and now, snugly holed in at Petersham, it was caught with its guards down. At nine in the morning when the forward units, themselves fitter for succor than for fight, surprised Shays' outposts, Shays' men were still asleep in haymows or featherbeds, or sitting at breakfast before kitchen fireplaces. When the incredible news came to them of Lincoln's approach, instead of rallying, they ran.

"Run into the house! Tell them to parade in a minute! The enemy are upon us!" one officer shouted to a ten-year-old boy. The lad, though scared of insurgents, turned to obey, only to find his father's uninvited guests in as "much confusion as a hive of bees swarming." They fled, as nearly everyone fled, Shays not excepted, through the back yards to the only retreat left open, the road to Athol. Some of them dropped their guns in their haste, and the Willard boy looked on enviously while his elder brother made a prize of one.

Lincoln's troops warmed themselves at fires precipitately abandoned by Shays' men, ate up the bacon and eggs and johnny cakes the latter had been preparing, and expressed virtuous indignation at the way in which insurgents had been "picking the pockets" of the townsfolk without offering compensation. When they were rested, Lincoln drew them up for an address of congratulation. Its terms were formal; like majesty, he referred to himself in the third person; but its tone was warm.

"It is impossible for him to describe the anxiety he felt during most of the time for the safety of his troops, endangered by the unclemency of the weather and the great fatigue they unavoidably suffered in marching through deep snow in a most violent storm in a country where cover could not be obtained," he said. "The patience and alacrity discovered on this occasion cannot be exceeded in point of merit but by the noble, virtuous principles which stimulated them to action."

Well he might have been anxious. Though not a shot had been fired by the insurgents, or a casualty incurred on either side, casualties were to come by delayed action. Already young Ensign Pyncheon, like many others, was finding it difficult to stand at attention on frostbitten feet. Others had suffered so much from exposure on that wicked night that they returned to the safety of their homes only to die of pneumonia. One was the seventeen-year-old James Sullivan, Jr., Harvard 1786, eldest son of the distinguished Massachusetts jurist and nephew of New Hampshire's governor.

Some 150 prisoners had been picked up in Petersham. Since most of them were privates, to whom Lincoln had personally promised recommendation for clemency, they were put on parole and sent home. Some who lived at a distance were furnished with provision and sleighs. "Their eyes filled with tears of joy and gratitude," remarked Parks Holland, "and they departed . . . completely happy . . . the last men that would raise their hands a second time against government."

The last observation was not completely accurate.

Shays' general staff had got away. Even Abraham Gale, though badly hurt by a kick from Shays' horse, was seen at Warwick, following the leader into New Hampshire. Lincoln's men were in no condition for immediate pursuit, and in New Hampshire the long arm of Governor Sullivan could be counted on to make life untenable for refugees of this sort.

But some officers were picked up later. In Princeton, Henry Gale hadn't yet nerved himself to give himself up to the authorities when the authorities came for him. In Pelham someone recognized a conspicuous figure of Shays' first assault on Springfield, Henry McCullough. His mother, Sarah, wept when they took him. "He had no father to counsel him," she told her neighbors, "and a mother who did not know how."

CHAPTER XII

Blood on the Snow

ๆๆ

No one in Boston could remember a time in the Revolution when there had been so much anxiety and suspense as in those days when Lincoln's army and Shays' were poised a dozen miles apart. No rumor, however fantastic, seemed wholly incredible. No one hereabouts had seen the rags, the gauntness, the scantiness of equipment of Shays' men. Surely men who had dared march on the Federal arsenal were armed for the adventure, and whatever they lacked would be supplied by their attentive British allies.

At this time a private sorrow merged with the general misery. On the last day of January, John Hancock's nine-year-old boy, his only child, trying out a new pair of skates, killed himself in a tumble on the ice. Hancock, long ailing, else he would have been governor instead of that idiot Bowdoin — such was a frequent opinion of the earnestly well-intentioned Governor — was wasted in grief and now might never be able to serve the people who so desperately needed him.

But General Court, for what it was worth, was assembling again. The new session should have opened on January 31, but in the disorganization of the times it could not muster a quorum so early. It was late afternoon of

146

February 3 before the House and Senate listened in joint
session to the Governor's message.

Boston at large, including its most substantial citizens,
also repaired to the State House. But there a shock
awaited them: Governor Bowdoin had ordered the gal-
leries closed. Only the legislators were allowed to hear at
first hand his militant address.

Many of them would gladly have surrendered their
seats, for they were not happy men — above all, not in the
House. One of the latter, Moses Harvey, was about to be
expelled and placed on trial for sedition, and many of his
fellows might have said: "There but for the grace of God
go I." If according to Holy Writ that man who lusteth in
his heart after a woman is guilty equally with him who is
taken in the act, how guilty were those whose sentiments
had been identical with Harvey's but had not been so publicly expressed or at least reported when expressed. Their
ministers could have told them, and since most ministers
were firmly on the side of the *status quo,* they probably
had.

"No neutral characters should be allowed, nor anyone
suffered to vibrate between the two," the frail, tubercular
Governor was reading from his notes. He need not look
up to catch the eyes of legislators who had so sinned. They
were conscious of a more searching eye, the eye of God.

Yet who but God could have foretold that what they
and their constituents had conceived as mere protest and
demonstration would culminate in open warfare? How
had it happened? How could it have happened without
the machinations of those foreign influences of which they
had been told but in which they had never believed?

Those who a few months back had been obstructive, debating interminably, delaying as long as they dared those
measures which Bowdoin had pronounced most urgent,

were now suddenly docile. Whoever spoke with authority, James Bowdoin or his right-hand man Sam Adams, him they would obey. What was asked would be given, and given with a unanimity unprecedented in Massachusetts. By the time they had been in session three weeks, James Sullivan, hardly a Shays man, was exasperated by their very biddability.

"As there is no opposition it would be a wonder if the constitution was strictly adhered to. And yet the critical situation of the Commonwealth requires circumspection in order that good men may not be made enemies of the government. The powers of government are so united in the metropolis that it is dangerous to be silent. A man is accused of rebellion if he does not loudly approve every measure as prudent, necessary, wise and constitutional. God knows where all will end."

In this mood, as dangerous to the welfare of the Commonwealth as sedition itself, General Court ratified measures nearly as fast as they were presented them.

On February 3 the Governor described the course of the rebellion and asked approval of his methods of subduing it, asked for an appropriation to repay the loans of private businessmen to government, and asked for an extended enlistment of the militia.

Next day the Legislature authorized Bowdoin to earmark £40,000 from the collection of excise and impost for repayment of the loan and support of the militia, and this without debate, apparently without even inquiry as to how such an appropriation would complicate the taxes, one of the principal grounds of grievance.

On the same day they ratified with the same frantic celerity an address drawn up in the Senate by Sam Adams. This expressed the "entire satisfaction" felt by the Legislature in the measures the Governor had "been pleased to take pursuant to the powers vested in you by the constitution for the subduing of the turbulent spirit which has too long insulted the government of the Commonwealth, prostrated the courts of law and justice . . . and threatened the overthrow of the constitution itself. . . .

"And in order that your excellency may be possessed of the *full* powers of the constitution to effect these great purposes, the General Court have thought it highly necessary after mature deliberation" — mature was for the House at least not quite the word — "to declare that a rebellion exists within this commonwealth."

All this on February 4, which was Sunday. "The danger the state is in," remarked Sullivan, "claims holy time for exertion." It did indeed, as Lincoln's army, now in Petersham, was well aware. Shays' followers, being pious men, had not looked for such desecration of the Sabbath, and that was perhaps why they had slept so late.

Only on two matters was there delay. One was Adams's resolution of February 5 that Congress be formally notified of the state of rebellion; this was ratified by the House on February 9, but not without some expression of misgiving about the risks of opening the way to "foreign" invasion. The other was a bill providing amnesty for the less guilty of the rebels, a complicated matter which could not be settled without taking action on nearly a dozen town petitions, including the one from Pelham signed by Francis Stone.

The latter was handled first. Sam Adams headed the Senate committee which drafted a reply, ratified by the House as soon as they saw it. The petition was rejected on the grounds that its authority was undefined, its tone self-justifying, "the applicants appearing to view themselves as equal if not better standing than the Legislature," and because of its blackmailing threat of bloodshed if not granted.

Most of the town petitions antedated the crisis of rebellion, but nearly all asked unconditional pardon for the rebels. "Many of them," Barre had written on January 18, "have fought in the glorious cause of their country in the late war and on that account are warm in the affections of their fellow citizens." Colrain, five days after the attack on the arsenal, deplored the recourse to arms, but observed that many respectable people had taken that recourse, and asked that the militia be dismissed.

Rehoboth, moving counterclockwise to the rest of cowed Bristol County, which now repented even its part in the conventions, as late as February 5 demanded recall of the state troops and pardon for everybody. It too deplored violence "as not only wasting the lives, which is the dearest jewels, but the property also of our commonwealth" with the result of making it still more difficult to discharge the "just debts" of the late war. Since to this date only the government troops had drawn blood or levied on the treasury of the Commonwealth, the sympathies of the people of Rehoboth were not veiled.

On February 4 the Legislature, acting on General Lincoln's recommendation, voted clemency for such insurgents as "may not have considered the evil nature and tendency of their crime." This would apply only to privates and noncommissioned officers who delivered up their arms and took the oath, with such exceptions as the general judged expedient. But on February 9 Legislature endorsed a proclamation by Bowdoin making it plain that there would be no general pardon. A price was set on the head of the leaders: £150 for Shays, £100 each for Luke Day, Adam Wheeler, and Eli Parsons.

By February 16 the terms of the amnesty to apply to
the rank and file of the insurgents had been completed.
They granted pardon, but only on severe conditions: after
they took the oath of allegiance, applicants must prove
themselves by three years of good behavior, during which
they were not to serve as jurors, hold any kind of office,
teach school, sell liquor, or vote for any civil or military
officers.

That such a bill would disenfranchise whole towns
either escaped the attention of Sam Adams, who took the
lead in framing it, or he considered the wholesale disenfranchisement of the hotbeds of sedition as desirable and
just.

2.

On February 6 Bowdoin was able to announce good
news: Lincoln's remarkable march and the breaking of the
back of rebellion in Hampshire County. It became possible, to everyone's relief, to reduce the cost of law enforce-
ment by disbanding all but fifteen hundred of Lincoln's
troops. Those that he let go, according to some of the
Salem militia, who were home again by February 10,
were the ones without proper shoes. Some of these, as
scantily supplied as Shays' men, were said to have begged
and pilfered on the road home.

Lincoln moved on to Berkshire County, where there
was turbulence aplenty; Shepard moved as close as he
dared get to the New Hampshire and Vermont borders,
and now the rebellion became an affair of international
relations.

After the debacle at Springfield and the rout at Petersham the insurgents had been "running their country" to
the neighboring states. Shays and an unknown number of
followers were in Vermont, "the new state," as James

Parker called it, anticipating somewhat. At break of day on February 5 Shays had been seen near Chesterfield, New Hampshire, with a hundred men in a body and followed by two hundred stragglers stretched raggedly over a distance of ten miles. In their way they had made a march as heroic as Lincoln's; all of them by now were "miserable and abject" and badly in need of the good breakfasts they had not been permitted to eat in Petersham.

Later in the morning Shays, giving up his attempt to keep his army together, sent word down the line that "each man must take care of himself." Two days later he crossed the Connecticut at Westmoreland into Vermont, almost unaccompanied. But Luke Day followed him closely, and Eli Parsons had been recognized in Hubbardston, inquiring the nearest road out of the state.

When Lincoln occupied Berkshire County, York State became the refuge, and, according to report, insurgents were made more than welcome in the border county of Washington. "Yorkers" allegedly had given aid and comfort from the first. There were hideouts in Connecticut, and even before the climax of rebellion, fugitives from Worcester County had gone into Rhode Island.

It was necessary now to deal with four governments. It was imperative — both Shepard and Lincoln stressed this point — to get permission for Massachusetts troops to follow the refugees across the several borders. But this permission was not lightly granted. Even Governor Sullivan of New Hampshire, who had experienced rebellion on the home soil, and who co-operated without waiting to be asked to the extent of supplying intelligence about the movements of Shays and offering to pick up any fugitives in his precinct, drew the line at admitting foreign troops into his state.

Diplomatic negotiation was necessary. Bowdoin began by sending his proclamation to fellow governors, suggesting that they proclaim like awards. Rhode Island replied first; on February 15 its Governor gave his unqualified endorsement to "peace and good government." But that was all Massachusetts got from Rhode Island; the Governor did indeed draw up a proclamation as requested, but his Legislature not only voted it down by a large majority, but invited a refugee to sit with them and watch them do it.

Pennsylvania did better. Benjamin Franklin, its President, issued a proclamation and sent a copy with a warm letter to Bowdoin. Pennsylvania had had painful experience with rebels. There had been the scandal of the mutiny of the Pennsylvania line, which in search of its pay had surrounded Congress in 1781 and forced it to leave town; worse, there was the tragedy of the Wyoming Valley massacre. Pennsylvania knew how to deal with the Massachusetts rebels, but, as it happened, it had none to deal with. Shays hadn't gone that way.

New Hampshire and Connecticut issued proclamations after due discussion, and so eventually did New York and Vermont, the latter with reluctance. Indeed, the attitude of both these states, whose help was urgently needed, long remained ambiguous.

3.

While General Court labored to evolve terms of amnesty, the tides of rebellion eddied in western Massachusetts. Rebels were taken; rebels escaped; rebels took the oath; rebels, hearing a clear call from one of their own, forswore their oath, rummaged in the haymow to find where they had hidden their muskets, and set out again. Though Shays in flight had disbanded his army, splinter groups remained to harry the borders, and across the New York line in New Lebanon, hitherto best known for its Shaker colonies, Eli Parsons was massing what sounded like an army.

"March all the men in your power to New Lebanon without loss of time," read an intercepted letter dated Partridgefield, February 13. "Bring arms, ammunition, four days provision . . . with snowshoes, as many as you can get."

To this he added a proclamation more fiery than any ever to come from the cautious pen of Shays. Would the citizens, he asked, support a government "which common sense and your conscience declare to be iniquitous and cruel?" Could they see the yeomanry "cut to pieces by the cruel and merciless tools of tyrannical power and not resent it even unto relentless bloodshed? Would to God I had the tongue of a ready writer that I might impress upon your minds the idea of the obligation you, as citizens of a republican government are under, to support those rights and privileges that the God of nature hath entitled you to. Let me now persuade you by all the sacred ties of friendship . . . immediately to turn out and assert your rights. . . . Help us to burgoyne Lincoln and his army."

Yet even in the full tide of such defiance the rebels remained what they had always been, worthy descendants of the righteous Puritan tradition, given to searching their Bibles and their Calvinistic consciences for guidance, shrinking from bloodshed, and not failing to attend Sabbath meeting even when what they heard there was contrary to their own convictions. That went for Eli Parsons himself, under normal circumstances the kindliest and most law-abiding of men. It may even have gone for those who, having under duress sworn an oath of loyalty to government, reverted at the first opportunity to the cause represented by Parsons and by Daniel Shays.

The oath imposed on the rebels was an impressive one: "I . . . do truly and sincerely acknowledge, profess, testify and declare that the Commonwealth of Massachusetts is and of right ought to be a free, sovereign, and independent state; and I do swear that I will bear true faith and allegiance to the said commonwealth, and that I will defend the same against traitors, conspiracies and all hostile attempts whatsoever; and that I do renounce all allegiance, subjection and obedience to the King, Queen, or Government of Great Britain . . . and every other foreign power whatsoever; and that no foreign prince, prelate, state or potentate hath or ought to have any jurisdiction, superiority . . . in any matter civil, ecclesiastical or spiritual within the Commonwealth except the power which is or may be vested by their constitution in the Congress of the United States. . . . I do make this acknowledgement . . . heartily . . . without any equivocation, mental evasion, or secret reservation whatsoever. So help me God."

Throughout Massachusetts, especially in the parts most vulnerable to government incursion, members of the ranks of the insurgents were reporting to their selectmen and justices of peace to swear this allegiance. Each had to affix his signature or his mark — and it is notable that few were so unlettered as to be unable to sign — and record his status as gentleman, yeoman, laborer, servant, hatter, or whatever.

But some were guilty of signing without due regard to the phrase "without any equivocation, mental evasion, or secret reservation." Since a term or two at country school had not necessarily included advanced vocabulary study, the words may have been so much gibberish to them. Or perhaps their casuistry judged that an oath imposed by brute circumstance was not to be classed with the marriage vow or the church's covenant with God. In any case, even in Worcester and Hampshire counties, now firmly subdued, officials were bothered by the many who managed not to turn in their arms as required when they took the oath, usually on the excuse that these had been abandoned during the flight from Lincoln. Some authorities would take no excuse: no arms, no oath. Others took a more gentlemanly attitude.

Sometimes the duplicity was exposed by acts of God. A barn took fire, and the officious found what they had suspected, an undeclared musket hidden in the hay. "A high caution to rebels," advised the *Hampshire Gazette,* "to discharge their guns before they secure them in the haymow."

Consciousness of such equivocation did not deter the rebels from attending to their devotions. In Berkshire the exuberant Royall Tyler, attached to Lincoln's staff, found Sunday meeting the perfect occasion for trapping his prey. One Sabbath morning he and a detachment of forty put a whole congregation under arrest in an unnamed town near Pittsfield.

When Tyler arrived, the congregation was at prayer. He stationed his men and waited decently at the door until the minister could finish. It was, he noted, a rightminded prayer; it directed God's attention to the virtues of government and of General Lincoln, and pleaded "that the heart of rebellion might be turned as rivers of water, and that these people might be made sensible that though they are careless and secure, yet vengeance might come upon them in an hour they thought not of."

The prayer over, Tyler, with a fine sense of good thea-

ter, tramped down the aisle past the staring congregation
and took his place in the pulpit. "That vengeance which
your reverend pastor deprecated is now upon you," he announced, and then, as he confided to friends in Boston, he
called his "sinners and marched them off with all the sang-
froid of a veteran." The sinners had come to church unarmed; they marched as directed.

4.

Such piety on the part of the insurgents did not preserve them altogether from blood guilt. During this
period of shifting loyalties, blood was for the first time
drawn by an insurgent.

The fatality occurred on the Vermont-Massachusetts
line. Shepard, now at Northfield, had managed to get a
Vermont warrant for the arrest of some of the insurgent
officers, among them Luke and Elijah Day, and had sent
Buffington over the line in charge of a party of horsemen.
Buffington ran into trouble at Brattleboro. Several score
of its citizens took after him when he set off toward New
Marlboro, and demanded to see his warrant. Buffington
retorted that he was after criminals and would take them
where he found them.

"No one shall be carried from this state!" said a
spokesman. "You are in pursuit of the most virtuous of
your citizens."

Some of the Brattleboro men drew their arms; others
made for the woodpile. Buffington went home.

In the evening he tried again, sending a small group in
"slays" after Captain Jason Parmenter, who was said to
have returned to his home in Bernardston to pick up some
of his belongings. This expedition had better success, but
at a price. In the dark, one of their sleighs ran into one
driven by Parmenter. Two shots rang out simultaneously,

one fired by Jacob Walker of the government party, and one by Parmenter, and it was Parmenter's shot that went home. Walker died half an hour later.

The snow was deep, the woods thick; Parmenter's party escaped. But Parmenter was not a man who could escape his conscience. He was known in Bernardston, where he held town office, as a decent farmer and a good father to his nine children. He remained all night in the neighborhood at the home of a friend and at break of day went out to inspect the scene of the collision. When he found blood on the snow, the neighbors reported that he wept.

Before evening Buffington's men, now on snowshoes, overtook Parmenter, his two sons, and a son-in-law, and put them under arrest. This time there was no resistance.

CHAPTER XIII

Cloak and Dagger

Royall Tyler was put in charge of the delicate negotia-
tions in Vermont, and, for all that he was going on thirty,
he flung himself into his duties with boyish zest. Even
General Lincoln, who had his hands full in the Berkshires,
smiled at the tone of some of Tyler's official communiqués.
And the recipients of his uninhibited personal correspondence, those friends who lived "near the ropewalk" in Boston, found some of it so irresistible that they didn't follow
instructions. "Put it in the fire. I am not joking," Tyler
would say in a postscript to a letter in which he had reported that General Paterson had "acted like a goose."

Two such letters were saved, quite likely by the ten-
year-old Polly Palmer, to whom he regularly referred as
"my little wife," and whom in fact he later married when
she was a bigger girl and he a steadier boy. They would
live in Vermont, to which Tyler was now enjoying a heady
introduction; after a fling with the literary and theatrical
set in New York, he was to return, settle down to the practice of law, and become Vermont's chief justice.

In 1787 all that was far in the future. Just now Tyler
—though carrying out his mission with competence, else
Lincoln wouldn't have left him at it—was enjoying himself enormously. Like many a government man of the

class whose privileges the farmers so intensely resented,
he took the rebellion as an opportunity for skylarking and
high adventure. To him the rebellion had overtones of
comedy, the rebels were country bumpkins, so ignorant
that they called themselves not insurgents but "sturgeons"
(he seemed not to have heard of the "Regulators"), and
their much publicized grievances engaged his attention
not at all.

His interest was in the sport of turning the tables on
the rebels and eying the "rebel lasses." He regretted when
he saw the latter that he had been eating onions. "I have
seen some very pretty girls," he wrote from Pittsfield.
"You had better come. You shall be major or captain or
indeed anything. I am major in the general family, but
colonel when I mount my horse at the head of a detachment."

Less than a week later, in Bennington, Vermont, he forgot about the girls while he applied himself to a man-
sized job. At one moment, he joyously bragged, he was
"harranguing Governor and Council and House of Representatives, the next driving forty miles into the state of
New York at the head of a party to apprehend Shays,
back again in twenty hours. Now closing the passes to
Canada, next writing orders to the frantic officer of 200
men in readiness. 'Mr. Selectmen, provide slays to trans-
port them at a moment's notice.' 'Pray, where is your
honor going?' . . . Will this make you laugh? . . . I
hope to be home and bring Shays with me."

To Lincoln, to Bowdoin, to Shepard, he wrote more
formally. He had occasion to write all three; his mission
was at once a matter of high diplomacy and, like many
diplomatic missions, a cloak-and-dagger enterprise conducted under military auspices. The diplomacy, especially
at first, was sometimes tedious and frustrating. It was the

cloak and dagger he relished. He was capable of instruct-
ing his superiors in the details of maintaining security.
An aide whom he requested by name from Lincoln was not
simply to announce himself at Vermont headquarters; he
was to give a password: "I have a great cold." When he
paid a flying visit to Boston early in March, arriving
somehow at the dramatic hour of 4.30 a.m., he at once
managed a message to the Governor that the "nature of
my communication is such that I could wish to converse
with you previous to your meeting with your council."
Bowdoin, keeping to the tone of mystery, arranged for
him to call half an hour before his dinner at two.

2.

In Vermont there was no question at all as to where the
sympathies of the plain people lay. The "rebels" had been
hounded out of Massachusetts by the iniquities of government; they were brave and honorable men; they could
stay wherever they pleased and as long as they liked.

In a sense Vermont was a state founded by rebels, and
its government a rebel government. Even Rogue's Island,
as Boston now called it, and not for the first time since
Roger Williams, was more respectable than Vermont.
Say what you would of its politics, Rhode Island at least
had legal standing. For better or, more accurately in these
times, very much for the worse, it was an accredited member of the thirteen American governments. Vermont,
pressing hard for recognition as the fourteenth, had no
such standing. Its government was the bastard of the Confederation; it held its territory, according to New York,
which claimed much of it, by no better than squatters'
rights. Its settlements were scanty, its roads rocky trails,
its people rude emigrants who had pushed up the valley,
mainly from Connecticut.

Vermont loyalty was suspect. It was not merely that during the fall they had enjoyed some commotions of their own, had stopped a few courts after the pattern of Shays. During the Revolution they were believed to have made overtures to Canada; Sam Adams had among his papers evidence on this subject. That had been during the period when New York had been pressing most vigorously for sovereignty over its claims.

Its people knew all about oppression. Their resistance to New York's claim was not due to any parochial prejudice against Yorkers, to whom they gave aid and comfort when they could, but because those same Yorkers could not call their souls their own under the patroon system imposed on their state in colonial days. Most of the lands were held in estates so vast as to resemble small empires. Necessarily they were cultivated, in so far as cultivated they were, by small farmers, but these were farmers without title to the land they tilled, with no way of getting a title, working as mere tenants, without privileges except on the sufferance of the landlord, keeping their homes on leases renewed yearly and terminable at the will of the proprietor.

It was not for nothing that Yorkers had worked with Shays' men and were now permitting them to muster a small army within their borders. It was not for nothing that Vermonters, whose history had been bound up with New York's and would themselves become Yorkers if the Devil's prayers were answered, were equally sympathetic. They could see for themselves what manner of men were running from Massachusetts — no banditti, as their enemies called them, but men as honest as themselves and perhaps more God-fearing, since Calvinism was less deeply rooted in this wild soil than it was in Massachusetts.

Wherever Shays' men went, Vermonters gathered to listen to their story. Their blood boiled at the story of the murder at the arsenal, at the tales of atrocity: Job Shattuck hacked to pieces, women and children mangled. For Shays and his followers still credited the exaggerations that had stirred them in December. They were in a poor position for impartial investigation — for visiting Boston jail, for instance, to see if Shattuck were as comfortably disposed as the Boston papers said he was.

Nor was this attitude confined to the common people. Tyler's first overtures to the Governor and his staff met with a cold reception.

"A pack of damn rascals!" Ethan Allen called the government of the sovereign state of Massachusetts. And he added that he didn't think it "worth anybody's while to try to prevent them that had fled into this state for shelter from cutting down our maple trees."

The occasion of this remark, though unspecified, was public, and Allen was cheered.

Governor Thomas Chittenden, though more discreet in his language, came out, according to Tyler, "plumply against our cause." He could not conceive, he said, that the offense of the refugees was such that "it was the duty of this state to be aiding in [hauling] them away to the halter."

This was the first spontaneous reaction on the part of officialdom. Later there was another. There had to be, for Vermont could hardly risk an open break with the powerful and hitherto friendly state of Massachusetts. Under the prodding of Tyler, both Allen and Chittenden were maneuvered into putting some very different statements into the record.

On February 27 the latter finally issued a proclamation as requested. It spoke of "the horrid and wicked rebellion in Massachusetts," denounced as leaders Shays, Luke Day, Parsons, and Wheeler (Chittenden called him Wheeton), warned all Vermonters against harboring them, and added that "all the citizens of this state are absolutely and most solemnly forbidden to take arms in support, or engage in services, or to contribute to the relief of the abettors and promoters." After his signature was a motto which in these circumstances might be variously interpreted: "God save the people."

The proclamation did not conform in all details to the Massachusetts model, nor was Chittenden's attitude even now what Tyler could have wished. The Governor had all month postponed this duty from one day to the next, irritably telling his Council that it was "indecent" to hurry him. On the eve of signing it he had expressed misgivings about its effect in impeding "immigration of subjects" into his state.

He was under pressure from the people; some communities threatened insurrection if he put his signature to this document. And even after he had done so, the Legislature protested that their approval had been restricted to the arrest of Shays alone. But the proclamation was signed, sealed, and delivered; Shays, however, was not.

3.

When Shays disbanded what was left of his army the day after Petersham, he made for Vermont nearly alone. Most of his officers, however, followed him by one road or another, their spirits, according to observers, "much exhausted and they said but little."

The ready sympathy and generous hospitality of the Vermonters revived them. Luke and Elijah Day frequented New Marlboro, where they had kin, and went about openly, flaunting their side arms. They were members of the Cincinnati and they liked to look it. Shays himself was more furtive. He remained incognito and took the precaution of seldom sleeping twice in the same house. John Hancock and Sam Adams may have relished going through the Revolution with a price on their heads and a rope around their necks. Shays did not. The prospect of ending an honorable career by death on the gallows was unbearable. For that matter, even Adams and Hancock, on the occasion when the British had nearly overtaken them at Concord, had run like hares.

In Vermont in later days, when fact and circumstance were forgotten, a legend grew up about Shays. He entered Vermont alone and lived out his days in the mountains as a hermit; one day he summoned the courage to go to town, but hearing his name called, he fled to the hills and died there. Like most legends, this one contains a measure of symbolic truth; like many, it runs counterclockwise to known facts. Tyler, and later Buffington, were able to chart Shays' approximate whereabouts, if not from day to day, at least from week to week. He was not alone, and he was too famous to keep up a successful incognito.

The presence of Tyler and his agents forced Shays' men to hold some of their conferences on the New York side of the border. Tyler heard of meetings at White Creek, where Shays had a sister, and farther north at Black Creek. To the latter place he sent three sleighs and "nine brave men," one of whom had served under Shays in the Continental Army, but the rebels had dispersed before they got there. A raid on White Creek was more successful; Adam Wheeler was taken. But "a mob of forty-odd Yorkers" pursued Tyler's men and carried off their captive.

The same day in Bennington, Tyler got a threatening letter. "Sir, your being in this town makes grate uneasiness in this state, and I would advise you as a friend to make the best of your way out . . . or else before you are eight and forty hours older you will meate with trouble, for there is 300 men at a moment's warning to take you . . . where you won't return."

Lincoln had a genial comment. "I am sorry you could not keep the bird," he said in reference to Wheeler. "You must, however, feel happy in having address enough to take him." And Tyler might come back if he felt his life was in danger.

But Tyler persevered. Mrs. Shays, who had been Abigail Gilbert of Brookfield, Massachusetts, had come to Bennington. He was having her watched. A Berkshire man was instructed to act the good neighbor and win her confidence, offering her money. The money was a mistake. No one but a government spy, Mrs. Shays must have reasoned, would in these parts have it to give away. Tyler got nothing from her.

By other means he laid a trap for Shays, this time in Cambridge, just over the New York line. A letter sent Shays suggesting a rendezvous actually got a reply, but not the man. Shays would, he wrote, be "in danger of depriving myself of my own usefulness by cuming to your quarters. . . . I should be glad of a conference but willing to wait till prudence permits."

Then there was a truce to the mysterious meetings at White Creek and Black Creek, and Tyler heard rumors about a Canadian expedition. At first he discredited them, but they were true. On February 28 Lord Dorchester in Quebec added a laconic postscript to a communication from Sydney: "Mr. Shays, who headed the Massachusetts insurgents, arrived in this province the 24th with four of his officers."

What were they after? Had their enemies charged so

often that they were in the pay of the British that they had gone to see if there were any substance to it? They could use pay at this point; impoverished, Shays was said to have pawned his own sleigh to make the trip.

More likely they were only looking for asylum. The traps Tyler had been laying for them, though futile, were many and nerve-racking. And, for all the cordiality of the Vermont people, there were symptoms of wavering on the part of the Vermont government. Governor Chittenden couldn't delay issuing that proclamation forever. There were rumors that he was driving a bargain with Massachusetts; if the latter would recognize Vermont statehood, Vermont would pick up and surrender the rebels.

The flight to Canada was at best a measure of desperation. For late members of the Continental Army to turn for help to the last refuge in America of the Tories must even in their own eyes have had overtones of treason. Had they been welcomed as they were in Vermont, had overtures been made them, who knew but that they might have lived up to their reputation.

There were no overtures. The arrival of this new and unsuccessful order of rebels interested Canadian officials not at all. Lord Dorchester mentioned their arrival in passing and then forgot them. Further details on their reception came only from Americans, some at a great distance. Yale's President Ezra Stiles, whose students had left off debating such academic questions as "Are There Witches?" to discuss "Whether Shays' Rebellion is Justified," heard that Shays' party had arrived at Ile aux Noix, whose commanding officer would "neither protect Shays nor deliver him up" to "pursuivants sent by Lincoln," who arrived two hours later.

A Bostonian homeward bound from Montreal saw the

party and identified Shays, Day, Wheeler, and Parsons. The *Hampshire Gazette* heard that two others of Shays' men, apparently freelance, had got as far as St. John, where they were laughed at by the British commander to whom they appealed for help. The *Independent Chronicle* picked up a letter purporting to be from Eli Parsons at St. John, which told of "many friends who wish us success . . . but we are destitute of cash or any other property except our clothes." A letter from John Wiley got into the *Hampshire Gazette;* he spoke of being "well treated by them which was my aternal [sic] enemies, which at the first appearance seemed strange," but "no stranger than my avowed friends to seek my life and plunder me in my absence." Wiley said that in a new war with Britain two thirds of the people would be on the side of the British.

Wiley, if the letter were really his, was writing from Vermont. Whatever the number of insurgents who tried their luck in Canada during the long winter, they all came back to Vermont and resumed the weary business of meeting at secret places, comforting themselves by talk of "beating up the bush" when spring came, of marching back to Massachusetts "when the leaves are on the trees."

Vermont was reasonably safe again. The Governor, having issued his proclamation, did not exert himself to enforce it. Tyler had left the state. After reporting to Boston, he had briefly served again in the Berkshires and then gone to New York City. His business was official, but, happening to see a performance of *School for Scandal*, he suddenly took to letters. He devoted the better part of a week to writing a play, *The Contrast*, and before the month was out got it on the boards. It portrayed the heroic Colonel Manly, who carried a sword presented him by Lafayette with which he had helped put down rebellion in Massachusetts. The real star of the show, however, was his upcountry man Jonathan, who confessed that he had once considered joining the "sturgeons."

"Since General Shays has sneaked off and given us the bag to hold, I don't care to give my opinion," said Jonathan. "But dang it all . . . Colonel said it was a burning shame for the true blue Bunker Hill sons of liberty, who had fought Governor Hutchinson, Lord North, and the Devil, to have any hand in kicking up a cursed dust against a government which we had, every mother's son of us, a hand in making."

General Washington received a copy of this play, read it with appreciation, and preserved it in his library.

CHAPTER XIV

The Berkshires

᛫᛫

Not visibly disturbed, his bulky figure sitting his horse at parade in Pittsfield, Benjamin Lincoln watched what was in effect his entire army set out for home.

It was only February 21. Neither New York nor Vermont had yet come to terms on the matter of fugitives. In the wild country away from law-abiding towns like Pittsfield, the hills still rang with "Hurrah for Shays!" But the term of the militia had expired, and Lincoln knew better than to try to stop homing militiamen. Cordially he wished them godspeed.

They were to draw their rations in Pittsfield and Northampton, he told them; to march in regiments and not "straggle on the road, as this irregularity would operate much to their own injury and the distress of the inhabitants to the dishonor of the army." He was thinking of the disorders that had marred the return of some of the troops that had limped back on frostbitten feet from Petersham. Their pay would continue until they got home. He wished them a happy homecoming and that "thereafter they may be free from intestine broils and foreign invasion."

Thus confidently and cheerfully spoke Lincoln, and not

at all like a general whose command in hostile country was suddenly reduced to thirty.

Again Shays had his opportunity. It hardly needed a Cromwell or a Cæsar to overwhelm the government men and take a high-ranking captive whose possession would be profitable in driving bargains with Boston. But again Shays missed his chance. On this date he and his officers were in Black Creek, conferring (to judge by their next move, which was to Canada) not on conquest but on sanctuary. His lieutenants, among them Perez Hamlin, in charge of the insurgents who clustered just over the border in York State, did apparently hear something of Lincoln's situation, but Hamlin heard and acted too late. His expedition gave Lincoln a wide berth, for by then the reinforcements had arrived.

"Those illustrious patriots," Lincoln's harried commissariat called the homing regiments when it saw what replaced them. Its staff officers had thought that they had had trouble enough with the patriots, or anyway with Lincoln, whose early days in rebel country had been marked by abrupt shifts in strategy every time his commissariat had rations nicely arranged and contracts all drawn up with local purveyors. But they didn't know what trouble was until the new recruits came in, men unseasoned by midnight marches over icy uplands, with little to do, since raiders in the Berkshires took pains to raid only those places where Lincoln wasn't, men who wouldn't touch the bread of rye or Indian meal that had nourished their predecessors, but insisted on wheat.

"Never was there such soldiers as the present," lamented Joseph Ruggles, worn out by victualing not only Lincoln's army but its prisoners. "They seem determined to do everything in their power to make me unhappy."

The insurgents themselves had been an army of strag-

glers ever since Petersham. Gone was the admirable dis-
cipline which had marked their conduct, as they put it,
with "a degree of innocence." Their ablest leaders scattered with a price on their heads, the jails of Hampshire
and Berkshire crowded with officers of lesser rank, they
were reduced to guerrilla warfare, to sporadic raids, punitive expeditions on informers. For some time everything
of a burglarious nature in western Massachusetts would
be attributed to them.

Their spirit had also deteriorated. From being crusad-
ers dedicated to a high end, however inadequately conceived, many had become mere seekers after revenge. The
cry of murder before the Springfield arsenal, when the
howitzers had opened on men who hadn't so much as
raised their rifles, had been expressive. Few of the men
who had walked so boldly into the range of the artillery
could have expected that it would actually be fired. In how
many places, Springfield included, had the government
men come over to the insurgents! Had General Shepard,
like General Paterson once in Great Barrington, asked his
men to line up according to the side of their choice, Springfield might have been a different story.

But there had been no choice. Shepard had ordered his
big guns into action, and now, especially after the debacle
at Petersham, the thirst for revenge was even more compelling than their desire to force government to recognize
the justice of their demands.

Sometimes it took mean forms. Barns were burned,
horses mutilated and slaughtered. Shepard himself, his
hands full with unruly Hampshire County, had been attacked through his most vulnerable spot. He loved his
horses. Not long ago he had pleaded with government not
for his own arrears of pay but for hay "or my horse will
die." Lately raiders had managed to work off their spite

on one of his horses, cutting off its ears and gouging its eyes before they gave the poor beast the *coup de grace*.

Small wonder that this general, who had almost tearfully reported the fatalities at Springfield, was now writing the Governor in a very different vein. The jails were full of captive insurgents, yet that fact had not so far stopped insurgency. Fugitives were sneaking back into the county to drive their livestock off to Vermont and brag that when the snow went they would march again. Men who had peaceably returned home and taken the oath listened to such stories and went off to join their brethren in Vermont. Shepard suggested a plan for relieving the congestion of the jails and pointing a moral. Would it not, he asked Bowdoin, "be prudent and convenient to have some of these capital offenders tried and executed immediately (if they deserve it) as an example to others?"

2.

Berkshire County was possessed of a spirit not easy even for General Lincoln to subdue. Close to the frontier in all senses of the word, and to the tradition of Indian warfare, it was natural for marauding parties to disguise themselves with warpaint and feathers. The term "Regulator," with its vaguely legalistic overtones, was seldom heard hereabouts; some groups called themselves "wood rangers."

The county's long history of insurgency, its refusal during much of the Revolution to be governed from Boston, gave the movement here a special flavor of right and inevitable conduct. In closing the courts at the outbreak of the Revolution, the people had been hailed as patriots. Now they were only doing again for far more comprehensible cause what they had done before; where was the difference? They saw none, and hardily went on rebelling as opportunity offered. Though the larger towns were prevailingly conservative, many mountain villages were to a man committed to the cause of Daniel Shays.

If until now there had been little military action in Berkshire (on January 29 there had been an engagement in Stockbridge, and several score taken prisoner by General Paterson), that was because so many had been afield with Shays. A Berkshire detachment had set out for the Worcester rendezvous in December and had failed to keep it only because of the snow. At the time of the attack on the Springfield arsenal, a strong Berkshire force had been encamped at Chicopee under Eli Parsons; it was Berkshire that had managed to get ten sleighloads of food past Lincoln's outposts to Shays' famishing army in Pelham.

Even now, with Lincoln's army holding the county at strategic points, and his scouting-parties spying on their very churches, impiously prepared to arrest them at their devotions, they did what they could. Mostly it was a matter of minor raids: ministers known to be praying for the wrong side were spoken to ungently; hysterical women in government households were instructed to "stop your damn noise." Warnings full of goddams were sent sheriffs.

And though government men organized more readily here than elsewhere into something like vigilantes, the people did not lack for friends in high places. Judge William Whiting had actually urged them to fight. "Better die by the sword than the halter," someone had heard him say.

Then there was General Paterson.

The general's sympathies had been ambiguous ever since that day in September when, instead of commanding his militia to defend court, he had permitted it to divide according to its sympathies. Since then there had been another incident. After Petersham, Lincoln on the march into Berkshire had been startled to hear that Paterson had avoided an engagement at Lee by agreeing with Major John Wiley of the insurgents that both sides should retire. This was when Royall Tyler had called Paterson a goose; Lincoln had remarked that he was glad Paterson had acted only for himself.

Later when Lincoln got to Pittsfield he got Paterson's less compromising version of the story. The latter had drawn up his 300 men before Wiley's 250 and was about to fire his artillery, when Wiley offered to disperse his men if Paterson would promise to use his influence to have prisoners tried in their own county instead of being hauled off to Boston like Job Shattuck. It was to this proposal that Paterson had agreed.

The advantage, as it worked out, was with Paterson. To be sure, Wiley made his escape and got to Canada, but when a day or so after the incident at Lee, Daniel Hubbard led another detachment against Paterson at West Stockbridge and ordered them to fire, his men refused. They would not attack a man who had befriended them. The result was that Hubbard was taken and ninety with him.

"They looked and spoke very impudently to everyone they supposed was on the other side. They halted a moment, and when the line of march was again taken up, they went off skipping and jumping." So reported an observer of one of the dozen or so incidents that gave color to contemporary life in the Berkshires. The men had, as a matter of fact, little to be afraid of. Even Lincoln had promised to recommend them to clemency, and since there was no room for them in the jails, they were customarily sworn to allegiance and sent home.

3.

On February 27 there was a real fight, the bloodiest of the campaign, and the prisoners taken were not so freely sent home, nor did they go into captivity skipping and jumping.

The stronghold of fugitives from the Berkshires was now New Lebanon, New York, due west of Pittsfield. It had for some years been a refuge for a sort of rebel, the Shakers, but their rebellion was of the spirit. The poor and heavily laden might resort to them too, but most were said to be converts from those who had already deviated from the ancient Calvinism of New England, the Baptists and New Lights from Rhode Island. Whoever would might worship with them in their three meetinghouses, join them in making a joyful noise unto the Lord, speaking in unknown tongues, and dancing like David before the altar.

Their community harbored an Indian who was said to be turning white and who bore the name of Sam Adams. And now involuntarily it harbored the men who had fled before Lincoln's army or who had mustered in response to Eli Parsons's war cry. These too sought salvation, but their ways were not the ways of the Shakers, who had left the world to find peace within.

On February 26, possibly hearing that Lincoln had been left nearly defenseless, some 130 of these insurgents left New Lebanon under the command of Perez Hamlin and headed for Pittsfield. But they were late; Lincoln was no longer defenseless, and a field piece they had hoped to pick up in passing was no longer where it had been. They changed their route, and on the morning of Tuesday the 27th reached Stockbridge, where, unfortunately for their local reputation, some of them forgot their military manners in the opportunity for plunder.

Stockbridge military stores were picked up and a score of prisoners, among them the schoolmaster, Solomon Gleazen. A less fortunate seizure was a Mr. Edwards's store of liquor, which some of the party elected to carry internally. Under its influence many of them turned to simple marauding. They made off with some valuable wampum belonging to Captain Jones, one of their prisoners, and ransacked the home of Theodore Sedgwick, whose Negro servant, "Mum Bett," acquired celebrity by decoying them from the family silver.

They paraded their prisoners down the road to Great Barrington. There while some stopped for another drinking-party at Mr. Bement's house, others attended to the duty of breaking into the jail to set its inmates free. Then hearing that there were government men at Sheffield, Hamlin's men turned west to the New York border. In the neighborhood of Egremont they were ambushed and routed by a party of eighty under Lieutenant Goodrich.

The engagement — the only one, as government men scornfully remarked, in which the insurgents stood up and fought back — was the bloodiest of the rebellion. Two government men were killed, one of them the hapless Gleazen, who had begun the morning so quietly in his schoolroom. Two of the insurgents died on the field, one succumbed to his wounds soon after, and Perez Hamlin, critically hurt, was captured.

Great Barrington, which earlier in the day had watched the insurgents march off with booty and prisoners, jeered when several dozen of them came back as captives. Some of the latter were very young: Enoch Tyler of Egremont was a mere lad, though by all accounts a wild one; Nathaniel Austin of Sheffield and Peter Wilcox of Lee, though both were married men and fathers, were barely in their twenties. Austin, as adjutant to Hamlin, had spiritedly led a small party of horsemen; Wilcox's brother was one of the insurgent dead.

Even some of the insurgents who escaped came to grief. The twenty-year-old Levi Bullock got safely back to his native Lanesborough, but, once there, dared not go to his home. Lincoln's men were scouring the country in pursuit of the remnants of Hamlin's command; if he were known to be there, he would be hunted down.

Secretly he made his way to the home of a chum, Thomas Mayo, who loyally undertook to hide out with him. They took a pot of live coals and a pallet of straw to the Mayo "potato hole," a primitive storage basement dug into a bank, and made themselves snug while another Mayo lad sealed the three-by-two entrance with boards and snow. During the night fresh snow fell, covering the tracks. Now they were really safe from pursuit, for when next morning the brother came with food, he found both dead of suffocation.

4.

Hamlin's raid re-emphasized the difficulty of controlling insurgency so long as pockets of rebellion were allowed to build up within the borders of the adjacent states. The tri-state border was wild and mountainous and full of natural cover for men who knew their woodcraft as these did. "Ten thousand men could not so cover the frontier," Lincoln wrote Governor George Clinton of New York when he first heard of the Stockbridge invasion, "as to prevent lurking parties from entering . . . over the mountains, plundering the inhabitants and burning the buildings."

It was not his first appeal for co-operation from New York. On February 22, after he had two pieces of evidence — Eli Parsons's proclamation calling on the faithful to rally in New Lebanon, and the action of the mob in White Creek in rescuing Adam Wheeler from arrest — he had warned the New York Governor of the consequences of inaction: "The disaffection to order and government is fast spreading in the neighboring states; the reins of government must be drawn up or they will be trodden under pretty generally in this part of the world."

There had been no satisfactory reply. New York, like Vermont, neither gave permission for Massachusetts troops to cross the line nor took any police action of its own.

The day before the Stockbridge raid, however, the Massachusetts Legislature had passed a resolution whose effects forced the reluctant hands of both the New York and Vermont Governors. It was a resolution that "the Commonwealth has been and is in a state of war." On March 7, after hearing of the latest raid, it implemented this resolve by empowering Lincoln to march his troops into any United States territory whatsoever "for the sole purpose of apprehending the leaders and others concerned in the insurrection and rebellion and bringing them to justice."

New York did not wait for Lincoln to take advantage of this enlarged maneuverability. In response to his appeals, and probably also to news that Bowdoin was asking for Federal intervention if New York would not oblige, Clinton and his Legislature took action. The Governor was authorized to call out the militia and to take command of any Massachusetts troops that crossed the line.

Lincoln, at least, did cross. On March 7 he held a consultation with Clinton, who had come to New Lebanon with his militia three days earlier. The result of this united action was that the recent invasion became the last large-scale engagement of Shays' Rebellion. The New Lebanon Shakers could enjoy their Sabbaths undisturbed by proximities to the vigorous young men from the Berkshires. The latter scattered — to Vermont, to Connecticut, and, when they dared, to their own homes.

New York officials became so enterprising as to ignore the Vermont line (which indeed they did not officially recognize) in the course of their manhunts. The home of Vermonter Josiah Wilson got ransacked by a Yorker officer acting on a tip that Shays was hiding there, to the fury of Josiah. "I am intirely willing to abide by the consequences . . . and tamely submit as a true subject to the laws of any state I belong to," he said. But he accused the Yorker of attempting injury to those "whose poverty should be your safety, they being poor and low in the world. . . . But sir, you'll find yourself mistaken, there being many ways whereby a man may retaliate if the law do not. . . . Suppose a number of the Vermont lads should . . . pay you a visit and treat you with the same freedom and politeness that you did my family?"

Nevertheless, the country grew so quiet that Lincoln asked to be released in time to visit his estate on the Passamaquoddy before April 1. Berkshire people were urging him to return if he went at all, the general admitted, "but I do not think that a matter of so much importance as they seem to." General Shepard, still uneasily patrolling Hampshire County, considered the remark flippant. Lincoln was allowed to go, but he had to come back.

The border situation, though under control, remained potentially explosive through the spring. Even the people of New Hampshire were reported "warmly attached to Shays and his party." The prevailing Vermont attitude made the Governor's proclamation a dead letter. "Shrewd, wise people had too thorough a knowledge of their own political interest and the oppression the insurgents had suffered to make any concern in adding to their misfortune." So spoke a legislator in Royall Tyler's hearing, and the Vermont Legislature managed to adjourn without taking any action on Massachusetts's request to be allowed to send in an armed guard.

Minor disorders continued. The home of the deputy sheriff of Pittsfield was raided and all the legal papers found there were destroyed. Jails were broken into and prisoners borne off. Half a dozen armed men burglarized Egremont, among them two "youngerly men" named John Bly and Charles Rose.

But most of the insurgent country had settled down in hushed tension to await the outcome of the trials of those prisoners who had been held for the grand jury. While they impended, there was little talk of grievances, except from Lincoln's army, which found a new one daily, or whenever they were offered cornbread instead of wheat, New England rum instead of Barbados, pork instead of beef.

CHAPTER XV

Spring Elections

The rebellion winter had been one of the stormiest in memory, with new blizzards crowding on the heels of the last. March came in with the usual bitter northeaster, and snow drifting to the attic windows. But during the month the back of the winter was broken. The thaws came; even in the night one heard the dripping from the eaves and the gurgling of brooks newly released from their coats of mail. By the middle of the month the land began to swim to the surface in small naked patches of brown earth, and farmers checked their gear for plowing.

Sap rose in the trees; the brush of the swamps took on the subtle glow of mahogany and chartreuse that precede the budding and leafing. The children brought pussy willows into the kitchens and followed their older brothers into the sugar bush. Throughout New England began the tapping of the maples, the boiling of the sap in black caldrons until it turned sweet and brown, better than any molasses from Barbados. Then the sugaring off; no store-bought sugar had the sweetness of maple crystallized on snow.

Sap was rising also in the blood of the inmates of the crowded jails. There was work to do at home; what were they doing here? In March came a wave of petitions for release. No one asked for pardon; the trials were yet to be held, and the prisoners would duly return to stand trial. But in the meantime, instead of wasting time, why not go home and attend to chores?

Job Shattuck's cellmate, Oliver Parker, pleaded that "the season of the year is arrived which immediately calls for the labor of your petitioner to provide for the support of his family." James Goulding said he was "suffering by being kept from the profession of tanning and curing of leather at this particular season of the year." Moreover, he had "left a young family of children at home, and a tender wife who hourly expected the labor and pains peculiarly incident to her sex." Hezekiah Hix of Rehoboth acknowledged that he had acted "contrary to the laws of God," but that his sick wife needed him.

Brigadier General Josiah Whitney of Harvard, whose inhibiting effects on the loyalties of the local militia and militant criticism of government in general had landed him in the Worcester jail, also pleaded the needs of his wife and children. There were seven of these, the oldest only twelve, and the youngest, Daniel (the name was suspect, for Whitney had a way of naming his young for celebrities who excited his admiration), was under six months.

Even Job Shattuck, the most despised rebel of them all, came up with a plea. His wounds, he said, were not healing in jail; his health suffered "for want of exercise and fresh air." What, authority might have asked, did it matter when the man was shortly to be hanged higher than Haman? But on the sound Anglo-Saxon precedent that a man who is to be hanged should be at his best for the ceremony, Shattuck was allowed home on bail. The Groton selectmen had endorsed his petition, and there was small likelihood that a culprit so crippled could escape.

Most such petitioners were released on bond or on assurance from their fellow townsmen that they would be watched and restrained. The citizens of Whatley had certified John Brown, a ringleader awaiting trial in Northampton jail, as a good citizen until rebellion started, "a man honest and upright in his dealings, and far from grinding the faces of the poor . . . [of] quiet and reasonable temper." Sheriff Porter and General Lincoln put in a word for him, and John Brown went home.

2.

The political sap was rising too. The time for annual town meeting had rolled around again. Very soon would come that event on which the insurgents had based their hopes, the election of a new General Court which would deal with their petitions more generously than the last.

The outgoing Legislature, which finally adjourned on March 10 (though there was to be one more brief emergency session in May when the state treasurer died), had not distinguished itself. Since February its resolutions had been almost wholly punitive. On its very last day it undertook to make life for the refugees more miserable than it already was by ordering troops in the western counties to arrest anyone attempting to move his property out of the state until he had cleared himself of the charge of treason, and proclaiming illegal the purchase of real estate belonging to fugitives.

It had tinkered timidly with a few "reforms." It had reduced the number of the sessions of the Courts of Common Pleas and of General Sessions, had made some observations on the payment of interest on public securities and on the lack of sufficient restraint on the state treasurer in drawing orders. It had also tried to reduce the Governor's salary from £1,100 to £800; it was only a try, for Bowdoin had sent the bill back as unconstitutional.

This General Court was done for at last. The time was coming when more courageous and generous men were to be elected.

How was it to be done? There were communities whose entire electorate had been disenfranchised by the last Legislature, and dozens where if the disqualifying act were enforced, only the minority in favor of the *status quo* would have a voice. How elect a Legislature closer to the hearts of the plain man under such circumstances? How, for that matter, hold town meeting?

Yet in most places annual town meeting met as usual and elections were held without too nice an inquiry into the technical qualifications of the voters. There were exceptions in the two counties still supervised by armies of occupation. In Hampshire County a dozen towns, including Luke Day's West Springfield, Moses Harvey's Montague, Jason Parmenter's Bernardston, failed to return representatives. Three Berkshire towns also defaulted: Lenox, West Stockbridge, Dalton. But Pelham, unabashed by its notoriety, sent Lieutenant Joseph Packard to the Legislature, and in general the insurgent towns were better represented than they had been in 1786.

Tyler on his way back from Vermont was appalled by the freedom with which insurgents participated in town meetings in Worcester County. In Barre he saw men lately in arms, and thus disqualified, not only participate but do it with bravado; they wore sprigs of hemlock in their hats, and one of them made a point of coming armed — with a wooden sword. In New Braintree he saw the disqualified vote friends of the government out of office and put rebels in their place.

Levi Lincoln indignantly reported that five other heavily disaffected towns in the county, one of them Shrewsbury, had met with an obviously preconceived plan. "They chose with an air of insolence to the friends of government and a vindictive triumph over authority the suspected and disaffected characters into office. . . . The old spirit remains."

There were symptoms of the old convention movement. Lunenberg and Sutton were trying to drum one up for the purpose of influencing the election of Governor and, by some sort of remote control, the senators, who were not elected by popular vote.

When elections came, Harvard belligerently sent to Legislature none other than Josiah Whitney, who had put in sixteen days in jail on suspicion of fomenting sedition. He was a free man by then, for when his case had come up for trial, no witness had had the temerity to appear against him. Presently, though in vain, he tried to collect damages from the state.

He was only one of the many delegates elected whose sympathies were known to be with the rebels. Why not, as Pelham delegate, inquired the *Massachusetts Centinel,* "the generous, the brave, the immortal Shays?" There was, it admitted, "a Tory and misled party against him."

3.

Who for Governor? Bowdoin, said Boston. Who had better earned the right than the unassuming philosopher who, with little initial help from his divided Legislature, had had the guts to take up arms against a sea of troubles and restore peace?

But was it peace? What kind of peace had to be maintained by howitzers? What about the humiliating figure Massachusetts was cutting with her appeals to every state on her borders to help her maintain order? "I have long been mortified by the imbecility and inattention with which our public affairs have been conducted." That was James Warren, a Milton man from Boston's own Suffolk County, speaking. The target of his contempt was as much General Court as Bowdoin, but people were saying that he was at heart sympathetic to the insurgents.

If not Bowdoin, who? Some names always came up at election time: William Cushing, James Warren, Sam Adams. But Cushing was a judge and of the hated legal profession; Warren, whose talkative wife Mercy, a blue-stocking, was in some ways more conspicuous than he, had in state contests never been more than an also-ran. Sam Adams? The father of the Revolution, the man whose writings had once been more inflammatory than those of Honestus, and who more than any other had stirred the whole state to revolt against unjust authority, now showed symptoms of political arteriosclerosis. He had in insurgent eyes deteriorated not only from the grand old days when he had led them all in bedeviling Hutchinson, but also from the time of the outbreak of 1782, when he had listened patiently to grievances, promised his help in redressing those that were real, and demonstrated by common sense which were not.

Where now was his courtesy and patience? Sam Adams was all on the side of the howitzers. He did not appreciate the compliment that the insurgents had paid him in adopting his own tactics against oppression. Committees of correspondence and what followed them were in Adams's eyes now permissible only to the Irish. Currently there was a surge of rebellion in Ireland; the Irish rebels were making use of such measures, and Adams was pleased. They were welcome to his invention; Americans who made use of it were suddenly traitors.

Consider for a moment all the fuss that Adams had made and yearly continued to make over what he called the Boston Massacre. It had long been in Boston a kind of holy day of obligation. What now of the more recent massacre? In Boston alien soldiers some thousands of miles from home had fired in self-defense on strangers; in Springfield a Massachusetts general had ordered Massachusetts men to fire on their own, not a one of whom had so much as cocked a musket. Was Adams trying to make the anniversary of this tragedy a holy day? On the contrary, the massacre had his approval; the perpetrators had his congratulations.

Such was the opinion of almost anyone with any sympathy whatsoever for the insurgents — that is to say, with perhaps more than half of the state. It was not in all ways a just or logical view, but while it obtained, Sam Adams was unlikely to get many votes for either Governor or Lieutenant Governor.

Instead of turning to the homespun citizen, whose ways were by choice as simple and frugal as by necessity were theirs, the voters were eying a man who lived high on a fine house on the hill, and had come by a fortune not by honest sweat but by inheritance. Massachusetts was looking to John Hancock.

Hancock could, as a matter of fact, have the governing of Massachusetts any time he wanted it. He had wanted it quite often; it was an office he ranked higher than that of President of that more tenuous political entity, the Continental Congress. He had not chosen to run, as the Yankee phrase goes, in 1786, because of ill-health. He was subject, among other disorders, to what his enemies and some of his friends referred to as his "marvelous gout," a painful affliction not deserving of ridicule, which had saved him and would save him from any number of embarrassments. It had operated like a merciful providence in 1786, for if Hancock had spent that year in Bowdoin's shoes, he might have been forced to make some unpopular decisions. As it was, the onus was wholly Bowdoin's; Hancock, his health improved, his impulse to lose himself in activity perhaps reinforced by his shattering personal affliction, could now take over with clean hands.

What was there about a man of wealth, a Bostonian with a house on Beacon Hill, to appeal to the impoverished farmers? The very fact that his fortune was inherited was in his favor. Had he built it up for himself, profiting by the war, he would inevitably have been associated with the sharp practice of Boston merchants, would have found himself in a self-defense taking unpopular sides. But there was little of the tradesman about Hancock, none of the sharper or speculator. He held public securities, but he had come by them honestly in his own right and not as a speculation at the expense of the original holders. Like George Washington, he had loyally held them even when they seemed worthless. Far from profiting by the Revolution, his fortune had dwindled. He had been generous with his wealth; the extravagant fetes that offended the severe republican tastes of Adams appealed to the common man, who liked bread and circuses as much as anybody. They brought color and gaiety into dullness. If such extravagance had lately brought Hancock into debt, it only made him the more endearing. Who were the insurgents but debtors, and how many times had they been accused of incurring that state by their extravagance in better times? Hancock, with all his fine linen, his brocades, his silver plate, his rare vintages, was one of them. He would understand.

So strong was the groundswell toward Hancock during

March that his friends had to deny a canard spread by his enemies. A committee of insurgents had made a deal with him, said the latter; they had promised him the job if he would accept their conditions: pardon and an emission of paper money. And Hancock had agreed.

Election was held on April 1, and there was no need for a recount: Hancock, 18,459; Bowdoin, 6,394. Bowdoin failed to carry a single town in the disaffected counties of Worcester and Bristol, or even in such apparently loyal counties as Plymouth, Dukes, Nantucket, Norfolk, and the three counties of the district of Maine. Suffolk, most of Essex, and Barnstable were his, of course, and although he lost the two embattled counties in the west, the fight there was close in spite of the overwhelming feeling against him on the part of the insurgents. But disenfranchisement had its effect there, especially in such of the towns as were now dominated by militant progovernment men who could be counted on to report illegal voting, and were of the opinion of Bowdoin's friends that if the election went against him all measures in behalf of firm government would be undone.

The results of the election were generally taken to mean that Massachusetts at large was in favor of dealing leniently with the rebels where leniency was possible. It did not escape the attention of some friends of Bowdoin that there was a way of turning the tables neatly on Hancock. No matter what mercy was shown the more innocent of the rebels, the more guilty would manifestly have to hang, if only as a warning to future generations. No executions had yet taken place, and Bowdoin had only one month more in office. If for that month the matter could be delayed, it would devolve on the merciful Hancock to conduct the hangings.

CHAPTER XVI

Condign Punishment

Joylessly the justices of the Supreme Judicial Court packed their saddlebags and prepared for the long ride into the Berkshires. It was April; elections were safely over, and the trials of the insurgent leaders could no longer be postponed.

The best of them were reluctant. The experience of most Massachusetts justices in the last six months had been such as to drive a sensitive man from the bench to take up the tanning of hides as a more honored means of earning a living. One of them openly protested their present assignment. Why hadn't Lincoln's troops completed their work? They could have hanged all the criminals on the spot by court-martial.

The point was academic. There had been no courts-martial and nobody had been hanged. Lincoln, far from relieving the judges of a painful duty, had doubled their embarrassment. Adding his voice to Paterson's, he had prevailed upon authority to have the prisoners tried not in safe, well-guarded Boston, but in their own counties. They would thus be among friends and the judges among enemies, among people who saw them as instruments of oppression, of a piece with the late tyrannies of the British.

Would they be allowed to hold court at all? Thanks to the troops, they could probably manage. In March the hated Court of Common Pleas had resumed its sessions in Northampton without, as the *Independent Chronicle* put it, "the *usual* interruption."

But they would have small joy in their work. The duty they dreaded most in Great Barrington, their present destination, was that of trying one of their own, Judge William Whiting. The judge had not actively taken up arms against government, but he had, if the charges against him were true, given more than comfort to those who had. He had encouraged, even incited his neighbors to the criminal act of rebellion, and now, like any other criminal, he must be tried.

The judges' apprehensions of disorder were not realized in Great Barrington. The town was well policed; the court opened without molestation. The men who crowded in to watch looked on in silence, waiting for clarification of that ominous phrase they had heard so often, "condign punishment." It meant exactly what they had supposed it did — death by hanging.

It meant other things, to be sure. For four of the lesser offenders it meant fines of from £60 to £100, and in the case of Whiting a seven-month prison term as well. For Perez Hamlin it meant judgment deferred; his wounds were too serious for him to be carried into court. But for six, all but two of them very young men, condign punishment was death.

The judges, who were William Cushing, Nathaniel Peaslee Sergeant, David Sewall, and Increase Sumner, kept the record straight by drawing up for Bowdoin's benefit a description of each criminal and of the nature of his crime.

The two older men, both in their forties, were Aaron

Knap, former Stockbridge town clerk, who had been taken in the Hamlin raid, and Samuel Rust of Pittsfield. The record of the latter included nearly every major disorder in the western counties. He had helped stop the Court of Common Pleas in September, was prepared to stop the Supreme Judicial Court in October; he had circulated Shays' letter calling on the Regulators to assemble in arms at Worcester. Rust himself had set out with a party of thirty to answer the call, though the snow had prevented his getting beyond Hampshire County. He had also attempted to join Shays in Springfield in January, and on February 27 had helped Hamlin's party break into Great Barrington jail.

All the younger men had been taken in the bloody Egremont action. They included Peter Wilcox of Lee, Nathaniel Austin of Sheffield, Joseph Williams of New Marlborough, and Enoch Tyler of Egremont. The latter was the youngest and guiltiest of them all. He had glibly sworn to his oath of allegiance days before he was caught fighting with Hamlin.

The judges completed their work in Great Barrington on April 8 and went on to their next sitting in Northampton. They postponed setting dates for the executions until they could get further word from Boston.

2.

Berkshire insurgents, who had stayed their hands during the trials to give the justices a fair chance to show themselves just, did not take the sentences with sweet resignation. "I understand that there is a number of my countrymen condemned to die because they fought for justice," read a note left at the door of High Sheriff Caleb Hyde in Pittsfield. "I pray have a care that you assist not in the execution of so horrid a crime, for by all that is above, he that condemns and he that executes shall share alike. . . . Prepare for death with speed, for your life or mine is short. When the woods are covered with leaves, I shall return and pay you a short visit. So no more at present, but I remain your inveterate ENEMY."

The buds of the trees referred to were already swelling large. Guards were doubled at Great Barrington and Lenox jails — with reason, for, according to the judges, three of the more notorious offenders had been spirited away before the trials. A doctor reported that Hamlin, whose rescue was said to be contemplated, was well enough to be removed to the greater security of Northampton jail. He was mistaken. Six months later it was reported that Hamlin could not be tried without risking his life. Wounded in one ankle and one side, and suffering "nephritic paroxysms," apparently he died a lingering death of his injuries without ever facing court.

There was not nor could there well be under the circumstances any open violence in the Berkshires in spite of the renewed turmoil of spirit. Most friends of the condemned confined themselves to lawful measures in their attempts to stave off execution. They wrote petitions; they exerted pressure by seeking out their public officials, their delegates to General Court.

In the meantime, executions were delayed. The judges, now in Northampton, had had a directive from the Governor's Council asking them to postpone setting the date until they had completed the Hampshire trials. And because Governor and Council were already under pressure from Berkshire, they asked the judges for a statement as to which of the condemned could be recommended for mercy.

In Northampton the judges sat from April 9 to 21, for the tiny jail was packed with no less than thirty-three offenders. The judges weighed the evidence against all of them, comporting themselves, as Benjamin Tupper observed, "with a degree of dignity which does honor to humane nature. . . . There is not a dog that dare to move his tongue."

The most embarrassing culprit was again not one of the capital offenders, but Moses Harvey, Montague delegate to General Court until the latter had expelled him for crimes which, as Harvey pleaded, had been "verbal only." He had, for instance, called his colleagues "rogues, robbers, villains and no better than highway robbers."

He had been picked up by Lincoln's troops in the dead of winter and sent to Boston. "His contracted position in the sleigh, and the severity of the weather at a time when he was unwell," reported Harvey of this expedition, "and the agitation of his mind threw him into a paralytic disorder." He could not deny his "verbal" crimes, however, and for them he was sentenced to a fine of £50, court costs of £16, and to standing on the gallows one hour with a rope around his neck. Fine and court charges were beyond the means of the unhappy representative; the other "infamous punishment," as he called it, was within his powers and presently he performed it.

Others were sentenced with Harvey on minor charges, among them Silas Hambleton, a justice of peace from Windham, Vermont; James Perry from Bristol County; Simon Bardwell of Belchertown, a notorious member of the conventions, whose activities went back to the uproars incited by "the noted Samuel Ely."

Six were condemned on capital charges: Jason Parmenter, who could not deny the slaying of Jacob Walker, though he insisted the killing was accidental; Henry McCullough, who claimed that he had set out with Shays for the first attack on Springfield merely for the ride; John

Wheeler of Hardwick, Daniel Luddington of Southampton, Alpheus Colton of Longmeadow, and James White of Colrain, all of whom had been indicted for their part in the assault on the Springfield arsenal.

These were condemned to death, and still the date of execution was not set. The judges were waiting on the Governor's Council, the Governor's Council on the full report of the Commission of Clemency. Besides, two more trials must be held before the record was complete. They took place early in May and resulted in two more death sentences: Henry Gale in Worcester County, and Job Shattuck in Middlesex. Job had on May 9 hobbled into court on his crutches to hear sentence in the courthouse where he had once given utterance to the "voice of the people" at the head of his disorderly legions.

3.

The Commission of Clemency, appointed on March 9, had been at work in insurgent country before the judges. Its members were Samuel Phillips, Jr., President of the Senate, Samuel Otis, and Benjamin Lincoln. The latter, thanks to subduing the rebellion almost without bloodshed, was its most influential member, perhaps at the moment the most influential man in the state. Poor General Shepard, without whose defense of the arsenal Lincoln might not have succeeded so easily, who had received small honor and no pay at all for his services, was, in contrast, a forgotten man.

Lincoln's views on clemency had been expressed in a long letter to Secretary of War Knox. Written on March 1, at a time when he had not yet solved the problem of patrolling the borders, the document was remarkable for its charity. There were, he had written, two bonds of civil society, love and fear, and to rule by love was best. The Legislature, by disenfranchising so many, by denying whole towns representation wherewith to work out their grievances, was undertaking to rule by fear in a way that risked perpetuating local "jealousies." To express fear of the electorate itself, even that part of it that had supported the insurgents, was impolitic. Even if "some of these very people should obtain a seat in the assembly next year, we shall have nothing to fear."

Lincoln was in favor of extending clemency wherever possible and admitting its recipients at once to full citizenship.

On Friday, April 27, shortly after the completion of the Hampshire trials, Bowdoin and his Council called in the Committee of Clemency and listened to its report; the issues raised were so many and the implications so complicated that they continued their deliberations on Saturday and did not reach a decision until Monday, April 30.

The report was optimistic. The committee had found the fundamental cause of rebellion in the prevalence of debts and the failure of members of General Court to instruct their constituents in the function of government and the purpose of its acts; instead, some of them had "by their conversation and conduct irritated and inflamed the restless and uneasy, and alarmed the peaceable, uninformed citizen." But the crisis was, in their opinion, past. They had succeeded in signing up whole communities to a revised loyalty oath, attesting to their "sincere penitence" and willingness "to defend the government by a punctual compliance with its laws . . . and according to [their] respective influence exert [themselves] to induce others to exercise the same conduct." The committee believed in the good faith of the penitents. Many of them were evincing a novel eagerness to pay their taxes as proof of their renewed allegiance.

The Council heard this report, listened to the committee's recommendations as to which of the condemned were most deserving of mercy, and continued their deliberations.

They had long been under pressure from people holding divergent views. For one faction Sam Adams, not a member of Council but a man whose opinion could not be lightly disregarded, was a principal spokesman. "In monarchy the crime of treason may admit of being pardoned or lightly punished," he had said, "but the man who dares rebel against the laws of a republic ought to suffer death." The Council owed it to the public "to inflict that just, condign punishment which the judicial sentence had awarded to the detestable banditti who raised the rebellion."

But Adams's inflexible severity was contributing little to his popularity. Even his part in pushing the disenfranchising act through the Legislature had been denounced in the *Centinel,* by no means a radical paper, in preelection days when Adams was candidate for Lieutenant Governor. The act had been called "repugnant to the constitution" and was said to have "embittered thousands and sent hundreds out the state." Adams himself was "fitter for a Venetian Doge than for the second magistrate in a free republic."

The opposite point of view was advocated by a disciple of Adams, Benjamin Austin, Boston rope-maker, who had been accused of inciting the rebellion through a long series of articles denouncing the legal profession, to which he signed himself as Honestus. In point of fact, Austin had taken a public stand against violence. But now he was for clemency. "Let us endeavor to heal the wounds with wine and oil rather than lacerate them with whips and shackles," he wrote in the *Independent Chronicle.* He urged officials to work to eliminate the divisions within the commonwealth; "those distinctions should be obliterated which have too long been inculcated between the yeomanry and the inhabitants of the seaports." What was needed was a *"national* sentiment."

Young Noah Webster took the trouble to write Bowdoin a long letter explaining just what to do. "Ignorant and seditious" the people might be, he said, but he never knew "an insurrection without cause. . . . The majority of the people are with the insurgents . . . in principle. They are *right* in their views of the domestic debt, although the insurgents are *wrong* to pursue violent measures." Then he demonstrated how the whole issue could be settled by calling in the public securities and reissuing them so that the original holders, not the speculators, got the profit.

From Philadelphia came to Bowdoin a warm, humane letter from Samuel Vaughan, commenting on the larger issues with all the philosophy of his friend Franklin. "With an education received under a corrupted government" — he meant the British — "licentiousness may easily be mistaken for liberty. For a just idea of the latter we must wait patiently the time of the rising generation which will be born and brought up under its influence." When even legislatures and "first men" go astray, "why then be surprised at the less instructed being mistaken in their opinions and practice . . . without the interference of designing men? The political maxims of these states differ from those of any state hitherto established, and the best educated and most experienced individuals are but novists with respect to their true policy."

Like Webster, Vaughan had a remedy. Philadelphia had recently founded a Society for Political Inquiry to study and debate the true principles of republican government. Boston would benefit by such a club. Then he went on, almost without transition, to describe an electric machine he had recently observed in Harlem. Bowdoin's philosophic mind had resources that sometimes lifted him above the frantic course of politics; it was good to have correspondents who could blend discussion of the dirty and possibly transitory state of affairs in Massachusetts with the clean and timeless course of the natural elements.

From Philadelphia also, in a newspaper article copied by the *Independent Chronicle,* came a view of the rebellion from the moral and religious standpoint. The troubles in both Massachusetts and Rhode Island were God's judgment on "their cruelty and hypocrisy in their being the author of the revival of the slave trade in the Southern states." Since peace, most slaves were being brought in by merchants from Boston and Rhode Island. "While this is the case a good man can hardly wish them a deliverance from their present commotions and distresses."

4.

Such observations and the multiple petitions already coming in from the friends and families of the condemned worked a subtle leaven on the minds of Governor and Council. A dozen had by this date been condemned to die, but the state must not revert to the hysteria of old Salem in the witchcraft days and have wholesale hangings. When recommendations for clemency were sound, clemency they would grant.

On the other hand, they would not grant pardons wholesale. Examples must be made to impress the present and future enemies of the state. The most guilty must hang.

They decided on what seemed a reasonable course. The counties most heavily disaffected would have the most hangings: two apiece for Berkshire and Hampshire. Worcester and Middlesex, being less subversive, would each be let off with a single hanging. The question remained, which should hang and when? The choice was made: young Wilcox and Austin for Berkshire County; Parmenter and McCullough for Hampshire; Henry Gale for Worcester; Job Shattuck for Middlesex. The date was set, May 24.

They had found the formula for demonstrating both the power and the magnanimity of the state. All other offenders condemned for capital crimes were released at once with full and free pardon.

CHAPTER XVII

The Quality of Mercy

After men have gone through the agony of irrevocable decision, have achieved it honestly by the light of their conscience and the best wisdom God has given them, they have won the right to rest.

Governor and Council had won that right, but they were not permitted to enjoy it. Their decision raised an outcry, nor was it accepted as irrevocable. From the back country in particular swelled up a chorus of protest. "If you're making an example, you've picked the wrong men," it said in effect. And the intimate connections of the condemned, the mothers, wives, sisters, fathers, brothers, cried: "If he must die, not now, not so soon. Give him time to prepare for his awful judgment."

The former protests were galling to the point of insult. Most of the press, the public officials, even the petitioners themselves agreed that there must be hangings. Governor and Council had given their best, most prayerful attention to selecting the candidates, yet now to read their mail one would suppose they had merely drawn lots.

It was difficult to shrug off such response because some of it came from very distinguished people. Theodore Sedgwick, who had come home from his post as delegate to Continental Congress in time to get hustled by the

202

Berkshire mobs, and had with Caleb Strong served as counsel for the Berkshire accused, was writing a series of letters about Wilcox and Austin. He wrote guardedly, disclaiming his qualification to pass judgment. Nevertheless, he passed it. Why Wilcox and Austin, said his letters in substance, when there were others so much more guilty than they? Why not as gallows mates that man of ripe years who had taken part not in one engagement but in nearly all of them, Thomas Rust, and the boy who had forsworn his oath, Enoch Tyler?

Since Sedgwick had presumably also served the latter as counsel, this was an odd suggestion, and it was irritating, coming on the heels of the full and free pardon of both Rust and Tyler. Because there were those who objected to the choice, was no one to hang? Certainly not, if Sedgwick's advice were taken, in Berkshire County. It was the only alternative he left. Implicit in the discreet phrasing of his letters was a burning moral indignation. What had happened in Berkshire, as he saw it, was that those who had the most influence in the right quarters had been pardoned regardless of guilt; chosen as scapegoats were men too young and ignorant to exert political pressures. They were men as likable as they were misguided; each had a family to whose anguish Sedgwick was not impervious, and which he passed on to Boston.

The plea characteristic of the kin of the condemned that they be given more time and then more time to prepare their souls goaded James Sullivan to sarcasm. He was not inhumane; in the end he himself would come to the rescue of one of the condemned. But he wrote Rufus King in New York that by an extension of time "the operation of divine grace might fit them for launching. . . . The work is partly done, but either through tardiness or some other cause," they want more time.

2.

The petitions that poured in on the Governor as regularly as the judges passed judgment and, unlike the judgments, kept coming with ever increasing urgency, presented a private history of the rebellion. The condemned laid bare the secret places of their hearts — with suitable editing, no doubt. Their kin described the anguish of having a rebel in the family. Their friends and neighbors offered extenuation.

Jason Parmenter's mother and his siblings, Micah, Deliverance, Israel, and Silas, could give little detail, for they lived in Sudbury, far to the east of Jason's Bernardston; they could only implore the Governor to "save the unhappy wretch." It was left to his own town and neighboring Northfield to complete the portrait. He had "acted the part of a good soldier in the late war," these said, and enclosed his war record to prove it. Besides his own service, his eldest son had been killed in battle.

His neighbors attested to his tears when he returned to the scene of the shooting and found in the bloodied snow evidence that his own shot had gone home; "this was before he became prisoner." He was of "hasty temper," admitted Barnerdston, but "not an abandoned character." His wife and children, formerly in comfortable circumstances, were "now almost ruined."

Parmenter himself made a statement, brief and without histrionics. He had been in Vermont and had returned to fetch some of his belongings. His shot had been only the "effect of surprise." He hadn't wanted to kill anyone.

By the first week of May it looked as if all Hampshire County were intent on saving Henry McCullough. The effort began with a petition of thirteen of the more substantial citizens of his own Pelham, including the justice of peace, the coroner, and a physician. They called him "a young man in the prime of life . . . the only dependence of an aged mother . . . although rash and imprudent in his language . . . yet far from an abandoned character."

The towns of Hadley and Hatfield petitioned for him. Ebenezer Mattoon of Northampton and Sheriff Elisha Porter between them sent three appeals. McCullough was "not the person to make an example of," said Mattoon, and his fate was universally lamented. His conduct, said Porter, "proceeded more from the natural levity of his behavior than from any malicious temper."

His mother, Sarah, said that she was "an old woman, mother of an unhappy child, my all, my comfort, my support, convicted of treason against government and state." She blamed his troubles on strong drink and questionable company: "Captain Shays, Captain Daniel Gray . . . who all belonged to Pelham and have been considered by him and others as men of judgment and prudence, have been the means of his unhappy fall. These persons he has been taught to believe and obey as officers in the town and have ever had the management of town affairs." She could think of several, she added tartly, whose hanging would better serve the state, but if her son could not be pardoned, might he at least be spared to have more opportunity "to prepare for that awful scene and not be hurried into eternity without preparation"?

On May 8 what must have been, judging by the number of signatures, nearly the entire population of Pelham, got together on a petition. It took courage; Daniel Shays' home town, first mover in that wave of conventions which had eventuated, no one quite knew how, in armed rebellion, had more present reason for lying low than for making itself conspicuous. But Pelham, as its bogus preacher, young Stephen Burroughs, had admitted, was by its own lights a God-fearing town; there were Calvinistic consciences there, and they would not let their owners deny an acute sense of responsibility for young McCullough. Their petition took the form of a vow. If he could be pardoned, the whole town would be "under the most particular obligation to use their utmost influence in the future . . . to promote and secure a due submission to government and obedience to its laws."

McCullough's own statement was that his part in the first raid on Springfield had been mere play-acting. He had planned to take the oath, but had been caught before he could do so. He was, he suggested, no worse than many others who had been pardoned.

Coming from him, Governor and Council may well have thought, exasperated by the ubiquity of that phrase, it didn't sound well.

Henry Gale blamed neighbors "in whom he placed confidence" for his crimes. He had become convinced in January of his wrongdoing and had gone home to Princeton "to submit . . . to the lawful authority and to the mercy of government," but had been taken on a warrant and carried to Boston before he could do so. Members of the three Worcester towns that had in January tried to dissuade the insurgents from attacking the arsenal, corroborated his statement, as did twenty-one citizens of Holden, all government men.

His parents, Josiah and Elizabeth, wrote a statement that no one could read unmoved. They spoke of the natural hardships of bringing up a large family of children. "We have seen some of them in danger, anxiety and pain, in sorrow, sickness and death, whereby we have been called to spend wearisome days and wakeful nights; but we can now say . . . that we never before had seen affliction."

3.

Wilcox and Austin had, as Sedgwick had reported, no influential friends, except, he might have added, himself. For some reason he had apparently made little impression on the Commission of Clemency, but through the spring he continued to send the Governor his guarded observations. He liked Wilcox for his bravery in action; "a cowardly traitor to me is the most detestable of all characters." In political ideologies "he appears little acquainted with any subject." Austin's father, loyal to government, was ill and so distressed by his son's fate that the execution would probably kill him. The young man had been only a private, and at twenty-two he had been married four years and had fathered three children.

Austin's town had petitioned for him, remarking that Massachusetts would soon be rid of the young man, since he had been planning to remove in the spring to the Susquehanna. But this town being Sheffield, one of the hotbeds of revolt, the petition carried little weight. Wilcox's father wrote of his "heart torn by affliction occasioned by the death of one child, and filled with the most poignant anxiety by the situation of another." But who was the elder Wilcox to ask mercy when his own insurgent sympathies had encouraged his sons to rebel?

All the young men had to depend on were their own wits and those of their wives, Molly Wilcox and Humilles Austin. The youths began by petitioning separately, but, becoming friends in the close confinement of Great Barrington jail, they ended by pooling their resources.

Wilcox's first plea was from ignorance. He called himself "unskilled in the true principles of government and . . . wholly ignorant of the rights of the constitution and the privileges therein contained." Like McCullough, he had simply followed the lead of those he supposed were wiser. Austin's plea was that he lived in a town almost wholly disaffected; he had resisted joining armed bands until late in the day when Hubbard had urged "a general collection of that class of people who before had been active . . . to prevent . . . hostilities between the troops of the government and of the insurgents." His explanation was oddly like the one Shays had made to Putnam. After the minor skirmish in January in West Stockbridge, he heard wild rumors of the severity of the government troops, gathered up his family, and escaped to New York. News of the Indemnity Act, under whose terms he as a private would have been eligible for pardon, did not reach him in New York. He first heard of it only after the fatal raid under Hamlin, and then friends dissuaded him from turning himself in, saying that he had disqualified himself. Never at any time had he tried to influence others; his sentence was just, but his penitence profound. Would there be mercy for him?

In May, when the day of execution had been set, the youths united on a joint petition with the probable help, judging by the rhetoric, of their counsel. If they were spared by the state, "our lives shall be dedicated to her service, and our now lisping children shall be taught to chant her praises and mantain her honor and her laws. Will not your Excellency and honors permit our youthful years, our wives, and our little prattling offspring to plead too in our behalf?"

The two young wives were in Great Barrington that day, which was May 8, working on their own plea with the same probable assistance. Humilles had sent in an earlier petition "with a hart almost broke with sorrow." She had described the "love and unity" between herself and husband "ever since they entered the marriage relation. . . .

The awful prospect of her husband's being taken from her in such an awful and ignominious manner almosts distracts her." By now she was ashamed of her touching simplicities and had probably been told that her plea was ill-spelled. She and Molly stood by while someone, possibly Sedgwick, worked up for them a document of more compelling rhetoric, and then the girls set out on the long trip to Boston to present the petition to Governor and Council in person.

One would like to know more of these girls. What part had womenfolk played in the rebellion? The only records deal with what they did after its back was broken: Abigail Shays loyally following her Daniel to Vermont and having the wit to avoid being taken in by the comforters sent to her by Royall Tyler; Sarah McCullough pleading for her boy; and now Molly and Humilles setting out for Boston.

But how had womenfolk taken the rebellion itself, the whole course of it, the conventions, the stopping of the courts, and finally the armed forays? With so many of the menfolk gone, there must have been double duty for women on the farms. To be sure, the climax hadn't come, and perhaps couldn't have come, until the essential business was done for the year. It is in late fall and winter that a farmer has time to read his Bible and his almanac, and to dispute what he finds there with his fellows. If a farmer ever has time on his hands, to study or rebel, it is when the ground freezes and the snow flies. But the livestock is still there, waiting to be fed, "bellerin'" to be milked, needing to be cleaned up after and the manure carefully preserved. Not even the Sabbath is recognized by pigs and cows and poultry. The management of the dairy regularly fell to the women; this year many of them for long periods had the management of nearly every-

thing. They had, however, been through the same thing
in the Revolution.

Berkshire women must have worked on the food pack-
ages contained in the ten sleighloads of supplies that had
caught up with Shays' army at Pelham. Women in Hampshire had the grim duty in the dead of winter of piling all
their movable property on sleighs, setting the older children to herd the livestock, holding the younger in their
laps while they drove, and setting out through the snow
for Vermont, hoping not to be turned back at the border
by General Shepard.

Humilles Austin had already had the experience of getting across the wintry hills to New York with her frightened boy husband and their three little children. Now with
her friend Molly she set out again, this time for Boston.
At least in May the snow was gone and the leaves budding
on the trees. If this had a special connotation in rebel
country, where all winter there had been talk of great doings when the trees leafed out again, the girls put that
thought from them. They were coming to Boston not as
rebels but as suppliants.

Their petition, thanks to the literary tastes of their col-
laborators — was it really Sedgwick, or had they got the
help of a schoolmaster or a minister? — was florid. But
that was the customary diction of the day. Bowdoin and
his Council were used to such phrases, and if they doubted
the desperate sincerity behind them, they had only to look
at the two girls.

Their children were "unable from their infancy to petition themselves," said their petition, but "will your excellency and honors suffer us at this early situation of life to
be widows under the most mortifying situation? Will ye
suffer our little infants to be fatherless and doom them to

pass through the journey of life, children of misfortune, subject to a thousand reproaches from the unfeeling and ungenerous? Surely not! Ye patterns of humanity, you will again restore our husbands . . . to our arms, and to our children. They shall yet live the monument of our country's clemency.

"Ye fathers of our Land! Yet, oh yet, let the sighing of misfortune, penitence and contrition prevail. . . . Let, oh let, not one rash action shut each avenue of mercy."

It's a pity that Sam Adams wasn't then a member of Council. In a nice way he was responsive to the charm of young women, never happier at home than when he had a daughter or daughter-in-law and their young about him. He could hardly have looked on poor Molly and Humilles in their decent homespun clothes, the sort he wished Boston would go back to, without being moved. Their plight and their plea might have relaxed the rigidity of his notions of republican severity.

But it was unfortunate for the effect of this pitiful plea that Wilcox and Austin were not content to wait on it. Two days after signing their own petition, two days after their wives had presumably set out for Boston, they took matters into their own hands.

There was with them in Great Barrington jail a friendly counterfeiter, one McClintock. Assigned to wait on the young prisoners and pitying them, he helped them break off their shackles and brought them bludgeons of thick ashwood to hide in their cell.

Before Wilcox and Austin could take advantage of these improved circumstances, a sentry, suspicious because they had approached him with a bribe, discovered what was going on. The bludgeons were removed, McClintock put in chains, and the condemned made fast. Worse, a re-

port was sent to Boston. Their honors of the Governor's
Council turned back from the report to the tearful petitions with a certain coolness.

4.

It was equally unfortunate that the insurgents at large
were not content to wait on the results of the petitions and
on the subtle influences being brought to bear on Bowdoin
from both within and without the state. It was difficult to
offer clemency when there was evidence that the rebels
would take it as softness, as fear of exerting authority.
The old rumor that when the leaves were on the trees
Shays would march again was still current. By late April
and early May the leaves were unfolding, and if Shays
was not actually marching, it seemed that he had it in
mind.

Vermont was astir again, and responsible officials there
were taking alarm at the renewed meetings of Shays men.
Judge Gideon Oliver of Shaftsbury looked in on a meeting of a hundred men and officers assembled in his town
to discuss a letter recently received from Shays. What, he
asked them, were they up to? "Driven from their country," they replied, they had met to concert "measures
whereby they might return to enjoy their properties." But
there was talk that these measures included punitive expeditions to Massachusetts to ward off execution of the
death sentences. Oliver told them that he approved petitions for mercy, but if they were hatching plans for violence they must disperse at once. They tacitly admitted
their plans by dispersing and reassembling immediately
four miles away at White Creek.

Captain Azariah Ashley of the Williamstown camp set
out for White Creek under the Massachusetts–New York
agreement, but the rebels had broken into smaller bodies

and moved farther north before he could get there. He heard news of a letter from Shays calling on his men to make ready, "for in a short time he was determined to have the matter settled." Ashley heard that men had been enlisted under the Shays standard and the date of their mustering set for May 10.

Ethan Allen in Sunderland was by now exasperated by these movements and writing that Vermont would co-operate with Massachusetts in any measure "which may be requisite for the mutual peace of both. . . . Your people may do well in the meantime to take care of private murders."

Berkshire County was taking fire from the rumors from the north. "They grow bold," Timothy Newell wrote Lincoln from Great Barrington, "and glory in being called Shays men." Men who had under oath surrendered their weapons were now mysteriously rearmed. Strangers carrying small packs kept passing through from Connecticut, headed for Vermont — to buy land, so they said. Over the York border a man hopped a ride in a northbound hay wagon and found firearms hidden under the hay.

Even Connecticut stirred. Until now it had been the least troublesome of border states; the lampoons of the *Anarchiad* were apparently more representative of the spirit of its citizens than were calls to arms, but in mid-May Theodore Sedgwick heard that in the little town of Sharon men were mustering into Shays' army. He alerted his brother, General John Sedgwick of the Fourteenth Regiment of the Connecticut militia; and the Connecticut Legislature authorized the militia to move in on Sharon. At daybreak of May 17 the rebel leaders were seized and taken to Litchfield for trial. They included William Mitchell and Dr. Barnes of Sharon, "one Tanner" of New York, Dr. John Hurburt of Alford, Massachusetts.

Their plan, it came out in court, was to march to Great Barrington to assist others in liberating Wilcox and Austin.

In spite of these portents the "formidable army" promised by Shays men did not menace the borders of Massachusetts. But comrades in arms must at all costs be saved. If armies could not be raised, guerrilla bands must be made to serve. By this means as the day of execution approached, two men were seized in Hampshire County and held as hostages for Parmenter and McCullough. On May 21 Captain Joseph Metcalf of Orange was taken by a band of twenty, and Medad Pomeroy seized in Warwick. Both were removed from the state; Metcalf was conducted to Brattleboro, Vermont, where he was turned over to Luke Day and taken to the home of his kin in New Marlboro.

At Pomeroy's home the insurgents left a picture of a coffin and a memorial in verse:

> *Now I have come, you must dy,*
> *And in my Bowels you shall lie,*
> *And if it's true what God he says,*
> *You'll be a prey to Daniel Shays.*
> *But before the day of June*
> *You'll think you're in an air by Lune.*
> *But whether you go to heaven or hell,*
> *I'm sure I cannot stay to tell.*

That at least was the way the *Worcester Magazine*, possibly of a more literary cast than the insurgents, reported the message. Both captives got away unharmed.

Harmed or not, the moral was plain; the sovereign state of Massachusetts was not to be blackmailed. To be sure, there were no executions in May. Governor and Council had already, with perhaps too little publicity for

their peace of mind, reprieved the condemned to late June
— that is, to John Hancock's administration. In Northampton on May 24 only Moses Harvey performed his
penance of standing an hour on the gallows. The extension
of time to the capital offenders, permitting them to prepare their souls, was all they could hope for. Hancock
would have no choice but to hang them.

CHAPTER XVIII

Act of Grace

Not since that August day in 1786 from which everyone's troubles dated had there been such a surge of movement from the country into Northampton. This time the townsmen were glad to see the farmers massing. Now on Thursday, June 21, they would see where sedition got them. The gallows stood ready on Pancake Plain, and at some time between high noon and three McCullough and Parmenter would hang.

The farmers came. Insurgents late in arms came and stared at the gallows incredulously. Was this really to happen? John Hancock, on whose mercy they had counted, had taken office; the new Legislature on which they had banked everything was in session. Would this Governor and this Legislature permit the hanging of men whose only real crime had been protest against what all of them had found unendurable?

Where was Shays? To what purpose had he been mustering in Vermont if this was to take place? Only yesterday they had been boasting that the Governor would not dare hang anyone for fear of the sure vengeance of Shays and his armies.

There were armed men in Northampton, but they were all of the militia with General Shepard in command.

Looking at the militiamen — all notoriously loyal to government — carrying rifles and ample ammunition, insurgent hearts sank. If Shays were on the way, he was too late. There were enough of their own party here to effect a rescue, but their teeth had been drawn when they had been made to surrender their arms. There was also that matter of the oath which some could not, after all, lightly forswear. What could they do now but stand hopelessly hoping while what was called justice took its course?

Since long before dawn the oxcarts and nags had been coming in. Men, women, children rode two, three, four to a beast, or looked out heavy-eyed from the straw piled in the bottom of their rigs. This time, unlike that day in August, the rebel young had come too, to watch the awful show at the gallows. And a good thing, reflected the townsfolk and visitors like Jonathan Judd. Nothing improves the moral nature of the young like a good hanging, and this would be more instructive than most. Children who saw what they would see would not grow up into rebels.

The first movement was not to the gallows but to the meetinghouse. The sermon that precedes a hanging may be the most edifying and awful part of the ceremony. Long before late risers got to the meetinghouse it was not only full but there was no getting near it through the crowd soberly assembled before it. There was, in fact, no room for the principals for whose benefit the service had been arranged. When toward noon the prisoners were marched from jail to church, smartly escorted by the guard, whose drums beat out the dead march, it was decided that rather than go through the awkwardness of clearing a space, the ministers would bring their stands to the windows and preach through them to the throng outside.

In the open, under the sun, Parmenter and McCullough listened to their last service. The Reverend Enoch Hale of Westhampton gave the opening prayer, the Reverend Moses Baldwin of Palmer the sermon. His text from Romans was bitter and brief: "I find in the law that to me who would do good, evil is present."

When the drums beat again and the march to the gallows was resumed, there were tears, and they weren't in insurgent eyes only. Nor were they for Parmenter, who was from far upcountry and little known hereabouts. He had lived a life already; he had killed his man and knew what price he was bound to pay.

But what of the white-faced younger man beside him? Everyone knew and liked Henry McCullough. Who hadn't seen him gallop his horse into town, making it rear when he pulled up to bring a shriek from the girls, who all had an eye on handsome Henry? He was at the very beginning of his real life, and now he was done for, undone by the like of Jason Parmenter, whose lead he had known no better than to follow.

What else was his crime? He had lightheartedly ridden his horse to take part in entirely bloodless doings in Springfield. For this they were hanging him while the real rogues rode free in Vermont. Hold the rope on Henry; the hemp had been grown and the fiber plaited in Honestus's ropewalk for the neck of Daniel Shays.

But McCullough, not Shays, was the one they had caught; the rope swung from the gallows and there at the foot stood the sheriff, waiting to do his duty.

2.

What would happen on the gallows had been the subject of earnest debate in very high quarters in Boston.

Governor Hancock had been discussing the matter with his Council since June 13. Resolutions had been drawn up and abandoned, papers read and reread, votes taken and retaken. All the crosscurrents of opinion, all the marches and countermarches of pressure that had beset Bowdoin now concentrated on Hancock. He had all the old tear-stained petitions and some new ones. One was a really sensational document. It came not from rebels taken and condemned, but from those still at large, and was signed in their behalf by the fire-breathing Eli Parsons.

It was a curious petition, all in one vast, non-stop sentence. Like others, it did "humbly pray," but expressions of penitence had to be looked for in extremely subordinate clauses. Its emphasis was on justification; its purpose was not only to save the lives of the condemned, but to win pardon for all those not yet caught: Parsons, Shays, the Days, Wheeler. It was an attempt to bring pressure to bear on the new Legislature, on which the insurgents had long been counting to resolve their difficulties, and which was indeed, to judge by its personnel, closer to their hearts than the last. In effect, they were saying let bygones be bygones, let us come back and go on with life as before — and meanwhile redress our grievances.

Its details had most likely been worked out in the recent mysterious meetings begun in Shaftsbury, Vermont, and concluded in White Creek, New York.

The petitioners said that they "did in the last year in a humble manner petition the General Court for a redress" of their grievances, "but failed of their expectation of obtaining it in a constitutional way, and being tenaciously jealous of an infringement on their rights which many of us in the late war with Britain purchased at the expense of blood and treasure, have had recourse to those means which nothing but desperation could justify . . . unwittingly shedding the blood of our neighbors." Some of this might pass for penitence.

"However unjustifiable the measure of flying to arms may appear to the majority, yet . . . common sense and experience hath taught [that] as circumstances of a people change it is necessary that the mode of distributing law should be changed likewise." The petitioners prayed that "peace and harmony" might again "pervade the once happy state of Massachusetts," that all members of the rebellion, including those "pointed at in the proclamation of the General Court in their last winter session as principals . . . with every other person of whatever description may receive clemency and return to the former allegiance as peaceable and quiet citizens of the commonwealth."

To reply to such a political screed was unthinkable, even if Parsons had furnished a return address, but there was an indirect reply in Hancock's proclamation, issued with the approval of the new Legislature on June 15. It was in part a proclamation of clemency. All men who had committed treason since June 1, 1786, would receive pardon except those "whose crimes were so atrocious . . . as to exclude them from an offer of that indemnity to those who have been misled and are not so flagrantly guilty."

The names of the unpardonable were specified, and the list was even longer than Bowdoin's had been: Daniel Shays, Luke Day, William Smith, Eli Parsons, Perez Hamlin, Elisha Manning ("of a place called Eleven Thousand Acres" — it later transpired that the name was not Elisha but William), David Dunham, Ebenezer Crittenden, Jacob Fox.

Automatically excluded were also the condemned. The

hard decision of what to do with them still lay ahead of John Hancock.

Was a pardon within the limits of possibility? The recurrent refrain of the petitions, "He is less guilty than some who have already had pardon," gave less offense to Hancock than it had to Bowdoin. The pardons had been none of his doing, and, besides, there seemed to be some justice in the statement. There was the fact that since the spring elections many more towns had instructed their delegates to work for a general pardon.

But there were anti-pardon pleas too. Euphana had been eloquent in the *Massachusetts Centinel* on the necessity for making examples. A general pardon, he said, would so inflate the insurgent spirit that men loyal to the government would be driven from the state. "Mercy, though a darling attribute and duty, is not at all times and under all circumstances to be extended to high offenders against the peace and dignity of the government."

How wholesome were the effects of the pardons that Bowdoin had granted? Some of the evidence was discouraging. Young Enoch Tyler, pardoned perhaps for his extreme youth, had left Great Barrington jail only to rejoin his former confederates. He had recently participated in a minor raid in the Berkshires, had fled again to New York, where he had been picked up on the charge of rioting. At the moment he was being held in Albany jail until a Massachusetts official could fetch him for a new trial on fresh charges.

Apparently clemency was teaching the insurgents nothing. Thanks to "the benevolent feelings of their forgiving souls," Euphana had written, "we might soon taste the sweets and solace ourselves under the equal and benign government of those who have risen up against us." What was left for government but exemplary punishment?

Yet Hancock knew that, for all his personal popularity, the bulk of his vote had derived from the widely held view that he would show mercy. After all, he not only had been recently a rebel himself, but had stood in the shoes of Shays and Parsons in that he too had been one of those expressly excluded from hope of pardon by George III.

On June 16, as a matter of form, Hancock raised in Council the question of pardon. The vote was a unanimous negative. Yet the Council did agree to a compromise, a position halfway, as it were, between pardon and hanging. Instructions were drawn up for the sheriffs of Hampshire and Berkshire counties. "You are directed and enjoined not to communicate the same to any person until the subjects of it are brought to the place where they were to be executed and then to make the same as public as may be."

In Northampton the condemned and the crowd that had come to watch them die waited at the foot of the gallows while the sheriff unfolded his paper. It was a reprieve to August 2.

"On Thursday last," wrote the *Independent Chronicle*, Jason Parmenter and Henry McCullough had LIKE to have been hanged."

3.

It was by later standards an odd, not to say a sadistic, way of showing mercy. Deliberately the prisoners had been put through every detail of the ceremony except the last one, had been nerved to the ultimate ordeal — and then let down. So was the crowd. It muttered as the prisoners, whose own sentiments are not on record, were marched back to jail. Even some of those whose eyes were still wet with tears for young Henry felt not so much relieved as defrauded. They suffered from interrupted catharsis. "The people," wrote Judd, whose eyes had been dry, "are much chagrined."

President Ezra Stiles of Yale, hearing of the matter two days later, was dismayed. "Should none be executed," he wrote in his diary, "government is not established and the matter will be all to be disputed over again by the sword; but if only one should be executed, the point is settled."

Henry Gale had also been reprieved. Job Shattuck, whose execution had been set later than the others, for June 28, was really like to have been hanged. On June 27 Governor and Council were still debating his case.

They had already spent the whole of June 26 discussing petitions in his behalf. These documents, since lost, apparently carried less conviction than those for culprits less notorious than that recidivist of rebels, the crippled Job. The *Centinel* charged that they had originated "not far from the head of the state, that a pardon might be granted . . . as consonant with the wishes of the people." The signers were "the lowest of the people . . . those who have been uniformly against government . . . minors . . . blacks." Insurgents were said to be openly bragging that "the government will not dare execute one. If one is hanged government will see what has never been seen. Shays and his party will join the king of England."

Hancock and his Council debated these considerations in the morning and afternoon of June 26. At last a vote was taken; Shattuck was denied reprieve.

But Oliver Phelps urgently moved a reconsideration. Next morning Council wearily went through the whole matter again. The outcome: reprieve for Shattuck, but not so long a reprieve; he could live on the government's mercy to July 26.

Not everyone took a cynical view of the reprieves.
Isaiah Thomas's *Worcester Magazine* approved; execution might have seemed an act of vengeance, pardon a
show of weakness; reprieve was a statesmanlike compromise.

Nor did Shays respond to clemency with vainglory.
"When the Lord turned again the captivity of Zion, we
were like them that dream." Reprieve was not pardon;
the exiles were still hunted men. Yet there was now hope
in the forlorn hideouts where Shays' men had cut down
maples to make them shelters. The Lord, who saw the
degree of innocence in their hearts, though John Hancock
had yet to acknowledge it, might yet "turn the captivity
of Zion"; and they were men who dreamed.

The melodramatic mode of displaying mercy did not
offend them. There was sound precedent. Almost any
veteran of the Continental Army could recall such "hangings" after court-martial. Washington had no prejudice
against a device which so neatly blended display of both
the might and mercy of government. Washington himself,
distant spectator of the rebellion, and initially so distressed by it, was by now reassured. He drew hope for the
future of America not alone from the firmness of government, but from the fundamental decency of the rebels
themselves. Their reluctance to shed blood had been
marked and consistent; never to his knowledge had there
been so innocent an insurrection.

4.

In Berkshire the drama arranged in Boston had taken
an unexpected turn. In making up their minds to reprieve
Wilcox and Austin, Governor and Council had been reading yet another of their petitions.

"Yes! Ye band of patriots, with whom our constitution

has wisely placed the sceptre of mercy, you will pardon us!
Your bosom glows with sweet humanity! The godlike attribute shall be extended towards us! Already we think
we hear the joyful news! The sages of our country speak,
'The cries of the distressed, the moans of the prisoners
shall be heard— *They shall yet live!*' "

If the bosom of Governor and Council glowed, it was
with exasperation. Suppose they did feel emboldened to
pardon this scapegrace pair? How give pardon to people
who won't stay put long enough to receive it? Wilcox and
Austin, alone of the condemned, had not been reprieved at
the gallows in June. It had not suited them to report to
the gallows that day. They still had no "influence," but
friends they did have, and the friends had helped them
escape.

On the night of June 15 a very young soldier, Abel
Holman, Jr., of Worcester County, and a private in Colonel Timothy Newell's regiment, had the duty of standing
guard at Great Barrington jail. The execution was nearly
a week away; it occurred to no one that the inexperienced
youth of Holman and his weak head for liquor made him
a poor security risk. Young or not, he was hearty and well
armed, and sentinels do not drink on duty.

This sentinel did. The jail contained, as was usually the
case if the inmates had either funds or friends, a plentiful
supply of hard liquor. Wilcox and Austin invited Holman
in for a drink, "and he being young and inconsiderate and
much fatigued with his task . . . partook so freely . . .
as to render him incapable of doing his duty."

Once Holman had relaxed into a pleasant stupor, everyone on the premises got to work. These included a sentry
placed at the other end of the building, who, according to
Newell, had been bribed, and the jailer's own manservant
and maidservant. The latter is nameless, which is a pity,

since she is the only woman known to have taken direct part in the rebellion. A file was fetched, the shackles removed, and then prisoners, sentry, hired man and woman labored to remove a stone from the underpinnings. When the prisoners were safely away, the stone was rolled back in place.

Now it came the turn of poor Holman to address petitions from Great Barrington jail, "this dreary mansion," as he called it. For next morning when the break was discovered, he found himself on the inside, along with the other sentry and the jailer's servants. But though the regiment was ordered out to beat the bushes "in six different directions," nothing was found of Wilcox and Austin. Not until after the day set for their hanging, when the news that they had been reprieved got about, were they recaptured.

In July they were off again; tradition has it that they swapped clothes with Molly and Humilles. They were out; they were in. Theodore Sedgwick quietly dropped his efforts at intercession, and authority wearied of trying to chart the whereabouts of the pair at any given moment. It would be good to have the matter settled one way or another. A hanging would do it best, suggested Sam Adams.

CHAPTER XIX

The Pardonable Sin

A lust for hangings was, however, by no means characteristic of Legislature. In the waning days of the rebellion, the insurgents had more and more set their hopes on the election of new legislators more responsive to their needs, and in the main their hopes were realized. Only a quarter of the old House, which had cut so timid a figure during the February-March session, had been returned to office. To the scandal of conservatives, the newcomers included some men suspected of making a direct contribution to the rebellion; Josiah Whitney of Harvard, for instance, came to the State House fresh from his experiences in Worcester jail. Such men were, however, few. More important were the many whose records were clear but who believed that now that the crisis was past, something more constructive than punitive measures was needed to restore political health to Massachusetts.

Many came into office with instructions from their constituents. Conservative Newton was impelled by the late uprising to express interest in a radical political innovation. Washington had finally reconciled himself to the inevitable and was in Philadelphia presiding over what came to be called the Constitutional Convention. Newton instructed its delegate, Edward Fuller, that should this

227

convention devise "a firm, efficient federal government on the equal principles of civil liberty, you will not hesitate to adopt it."

Towns closer to the heart of rebellion, inclined by temperament and experience to believe that the powers of government should be diminished, not enlargened, were generally oblivious to such apparent irrelevancies as constitutional conventions and concentrated on more immediately practical matters. Benjamin Joslyn got pulled and hauled by factions in the still turbulent town of New Braintree. Town meeting instructed him; then a protest signed by twenty-eight counter-instructed him; then a protest to the protest maintaining that the dissidents had not raised their objections in town meeting reasserted the original instructions.

What the New Braintree majority put first was a general act of indemnity "that the banished may be called home and not be as the woman of Tekoa told King David, like water spilt on the ground which cannot be gathered." (The dissidents, reaching for their own Bibles, remarked that Tekoa's advice to David led to the disobedience of Absalom.) They also wanted the abolition of the Courts of Common Pleas and General Sessions; the discharge of the present sheriff of Worcester County (they got this; Sheriff William Greenleaf was shortly to stand trial for malfeasance of funds); the continued suspension of the act for collecting private debts.

The delegate from conservative Milton confided his private views to John Adams. He was James Warren, elected to the House, over which he was to preside in spite of gossip accrediting him with insurgent sympathies. He had never seen the conventions as based on a desire to annihilate the state. "The people resemble a child who feels hurt and uneasy and quarrels with everything around him." He found no real system in their complaints. The government had been aroused from sleep into a "peevish disposition. . . . The people are irritated not softened. The rebels are dispersed but not subdued, and for fear that Captain Shays should destroy the constitution they violated it themselves."

He was more pleased than not with the results of the election, except for the return to office of his old friend Sam Adams, in whom he could no longer recognize the revolutionary firebrand. "He seems to have forsaken all his old principles and professions and to have become the most arbitrary and despotic man on the Council."

2.

Eli Parsons's petition for general pardon, presented on the eve of the "execution" in Northampton, had had some effect on the Legislature, to which it was addressed. The day after the "parade of death" at the gallows, the House took a first step toward pardon; it passed a resolution repealing the Governor's proclamation of reward for the capture of the ringleaders of rebellion.

But the resolution was promptly blocked by the Senate, which Sam Adams's Spartan notions of retribution still dominated.

Legislature worked on other attempts to restore life to normal. As early as June 14 a move was made to restore habeas corpus, though its suspension would expire on July 1 in any case. The Tender Act was continued, and Hancock with a large gesture voluntarily surrendered £300 of his salary on condition that this reduction not affect his successor. As John Hancock's successor, however, was to be John Hancock, the Legislature took unkind advantage; the Governor, who was little more skilled in handling his patrimony than Sam Adams, and might have been reduced to the same circumstances had not his inheritance been larger, was both pained and embarrassed. He was not prospering, and Harvard College was all but obliged to sue for the recovery of funds injudiciously entrusted to his management.

A pious resolution on the nature of the social compact was unanimously adopted to pacify the western end of the state. But not until the fall session would that Legislature get around to what was perhaps its most humane act: "An Act for the Relief of Poor Prisoners who were committed by Execution for Debt." This provided that a man committed to prison for debt only and unable to support himself there might be released on his taking an oath to his poverty. There were conditions: all his personal property, even that acquired after release, was subject to seizure to apply to the debt, barring personal wearing-apparel and household goods; and the debtor would be recommitted if it were discovered that he had concealed or conveyed any part of his property contrary to his oath. The act, however, was a marked advance and corrected at least partially one of the intolerable conditions that had precipitated Shays' Rebellion.

The fall session was also to modify that part of the disenfranchising act of February 26 which forbade persons concerned with rebellion to serve as jurors; it had to. There were too many communities where under strict application of the act it would have been impossible to panel a jury at all.

In spite of such concessions, the new Legislature, especially in the summer session which ended on July 7, did not live up to the more extravagant hopes of the insurgents. Punitive measures were not canceled; there was intense debate on the question of withdrawing the army of occupation from Berkshire and Hampshire counties, but the army stayed; the Legislature empowered the Governor to keep from five hundred to six hundred troops there. A motion for general pardon lost even in the House by 100 to 94.

An even greater blow was the failure to pass a paper-money bill. The experiment had been tried in several states to the south, and in South Carolina and New York, whose merchants pledged themselves to support the currency, with success. But Massachusetts was best acquainted with the Rhode Island experiment, which by now had come full circle. Not only had paper money been issued there, but through state loans it had been put into the pockets of those who most needed it, the farmers. Merchants and creditors had been required under pain of heavy penalties to accept the stuff. It hadn't worked. Creditors had been leaving the state rather than accept payment in such currency; merchants had shut up shop. Finally the Rhode Island Supreme Court had declared the act unconstitutional. The condition of the farmers, who had lately been forced to dump their unsalable milk and burn their produce, was not visibly improved. Even in Bristol County, where agitation for this measure had been most pronounced, many had lost their enthusiasm for following the lead of Rhode Island.

There was another reason for the ebbing interest in the measure. Insensibly, without anyone's knowing quite how or being able to take credit for it, times were somehow improving.

3.

The troops remained in the western counties, but already in reduced force. As early as mid-April the Federal troops, sent to Springfield on the fiction of controlling "Indian" uprisings, were dismissed. There had been protest from the troops themselves. Officers claimed that they had nearly ruined themselves by selling their stock at a disadvantage to equip themselves for the field, had even sent to Europe for proper swords, epaulets, and uniforms. Their men expressed wistful regrets of "not having an opportunity of seeing the fine lands to the westward."

Since the June reprieves, there had been little talk of insurgent armies on the borders. There had been no more organized attempts to rescue the condemned. To be sure, it remained impossible to keep Wilcox and Austin in jail long at a time, but this was a matter of connivance and bribery, not of concerted force; disorders continued in the Berkshires, but they were sporadic and came under the head of burglary rather than insurrection.

By August, Hancock was able to reduce the forces from five hundred to two hundred; by September 12 to dissolve them altogether. And on that date came also "full, free, and ample pardon" to such of the condemned as had remained like gentlemen in jail.

There had been no hangings either in August of July on the days to which the reprieves had been extended. No one seriously expected that there would be. To friends of the condemned the reprieves were now a source of exasperation rather than a relief. It seemed to them to serve no merciful end to keep up the suspense so long. Hancock was obviously not going to hang anybody. Why not commute the sentences and have done with it? But Hancock had his reasons. There were still many, among them Sam Adams, who insisted that the sentences be carried out. Too early a pardon would alienate such advisers. Besides, the suspense did serve a purpose. It enabled him to keep a long watch on the borders where there was still potential danger. Not until he was wholly reassured as to the situation there would he risk pardon.

Even then pardon involved some troublesome decisions. Henry Gale, Henry McCullough, and even Job Shattuck could be discharged with little discussion, but what of Jason Parmenter, who had committed not only treason but murder?

James Sullivan undertook to review this case for the Council, of which he was a member. He contended that but for the rebellion Parmenter's killing of Walker would have been judged "manslaughter at most." Even in Britain there were precedents for clemency in such a case. The government could not be accused of fearing to carry out the sentence, for the "parade of death" in Northampton "was so far from exciting opposition to legal authority that a gloomy silence and solemn awe at the power of government was universally felt." Those who had earlier advised reprieve were now under a "solemn obligation" to pardon if "peace and tranquility could be restored without public sanguinary measurers."

Sullivan reviewed the whole course of rebellion. Like Warren, he did not see the commotions as proof that the people were ungovernable; they had arisen from an "unfortunate concurrence of circumstances." Taxes, heavy at best, had become intolerable during the shortage of cash; the creditor-debtor relation had been complicated by the oppressive costs of the lawsuits and by the "sharpers who will improve the moment . . . of keen distress to extort from the wretched the small remains of property."

It might have been Honestus talking, not a distinguished member of the legal order that Honestus so despised. That thought evidently struck Sullivan himself, who hastily added that the price of independence itself had been mistaken by the insurgents for a grievance.

He returned to his main point. There was no current reason to suppose that carrying out the death sentence would arouse new commotions, but he saw no "public advantage from the execution of those people after all their sufferings and at a time when the state has sunk into the arms of peace and tranquility."

And Parmenter, honest man, who had essayed no jailbreaks, who had stood up that harrowing day in June to the supreme penalty, and who had kept Henry McCullough, who might have been his son, as steadfast as himself, went home to Bernardston. McCullough went home to Pelham, a subdued and chastened Pelham.

4.

In the light of not at all ancient Massachusetts history, the clemency shown the capital offenders was extraordinary. Not one hundred years before, a score of men and women had been convicted on shadowy evidence of the intangible crime of witchcraft and all had been hanged. The Massachusetts Governor of that day, under pressure, had not been able to honor a reprieve that he had granted. There was nothing shadowy about the evidence against the rebels. There had been hundreds of witnesses to Job Shattuck's misdeeds at Concord; it had not been necessary to invoke spectral evidence to demonstrate Henry McCullough's part in the raid on Springfield or Jason Parmenter's killing of Walker. One and all, they had been found guilty of treason. How was it possible that the government of Massachusetts, of all governments, had given them "full and free pardon"?

The answer was that, however tangible the crime, the government against which they had committed it was less so. The Commonwealth of Massachusetts, to be sure, had more substance that that most dimly apprehended of entities, the Confederation; but on the state no less than on the federal level, government was still molten, as it were, still in evolution. The old loyalties had been dissolved with the allegiance to Britain, and above the level of town meeting what had taken their place was still imperfectly realized. As the Philadelphian had so wisely observed, the new situation was without precedent in the history of nations, and all were "novists" in government.

Could anything worse be fairly said of the methods used by the insurgents to implement their protest than that they were in the new situation demonstrably impractical? Only yesterday every maneuver adopted by the insurgents — conventions, committees of correspondence, stopping of courts, even seizing the public stocks of powder and arms — had been regarded as acts of purest patriotism. At what point did patriotism yesterday become treason today? Sam Adams had an answer: the point at which the government of Massachusetts had been set up under its own constitution.

But that, at so early a date, was a pedant's reply. Who but the specialists had digested all the details of the constitution? Even some specialists had balked at its provision that it was not to be amended for fifteen years. What divine wisdom had empowered its framers to foresee all the exigencies of so many years? There was much justice in the plea of Eli Parsons, rebel, that government be allowed to change with changing times.

Government was not to be amended by force of arms. The inefficacy of that kind of textual criticism had been amply proved, and there must be no more rebellions. But now that this one was over, why perpetuate its spirit by creating martyrs for an ill-conceived cause?

Most of Massachusetts, reasoning on something like these lines, was relieved by the pardons. But approval was by no means unanimous. Sam Adams thought the policy mistaken. The *Massachusetts Centinel* marveled at the administration's desire to curry popularity with the insurgents; "the innocent suffer while the guilty triumph over the constitution and the laws."

In the *Worcester Magazine* Cato Censorious scathingly denounced Sullivan's defense of Parmenter. "What . . . all the sober friends of government deemed a high-handed, unnatural and unprovoked rebellion, you have justified by saying that 'taxes had become INTOLERABLE,' . . . and such (UNPAID) intolerable taxes, it seems, only produced 'some unhappy commotions which did not fix the characters of the insurgents . . . as ungovernable.' . . . Why now a'n't you ashamed to tell such a *Thumper.*" Cato believed this alleged defense by a member of Council to be a forgery. "To get rid of such a pestiferous creature" as the real author of the speech "is more to be wished for than the execution of a Parmenter, or even a Parsons or a Shays."

"There are circumstances where [mercy]," wrote another writer in the Worcester paper, "cannot be done without the most flagrant injustice." He cited as examples of it the cowing of orderly government men by pardoned returnees from the insurgent uprisings.

Rioting had subsided in Massachusetts, but contentions had not. Insurgent congregations were ousting pro-government parsons. The Cincinnati chose Independence Day for the formal expulsion of Luke and Elijah Day from its ranks. All over the state the current crop of boy babies was getting named according to the sympathies of their parents. Jonathan Judd named his newborn for Parmenter's victim, Walker; Josiah Whitney prepared to name his next for John Hancock; in Whatley on the same Sunday two babies were christened: one Benjamin Lincoln, the other Daniel Shays.

5.

The pardoning of the condemned did not constitute a
general pardon. The status of Wilcox and Austin was still
anomalous; government would not pardon them while
they remained unlawfully at large; it simply stopped sending out posses after them. Shays, Parsons, the Days were
not invited home. A lesser offender, the mysterious Elisha
Manning of "the place called Eleven Thousand Acres,"
was finally identified as William Manning. James Warren's House attempted to pardon him, but this move was
nonconcurred by Sam Adams's Senate by a vote of twelve
to eleven. As a compromise Manning was offered a pardon
conditional on his putting in seven years of hard labor at
Castle Island.

And in Berkshire County there was actually a hanging.
That the event passed off quietly, without jailbreaks or
attempts at rescue, was largely due to the fact that it
caught everyone by surprise, particularly the two principals. "Since my confinement in jail I have been conducted
as if I never was to be executed," said one of them. "The
many pardons that have . . . been granted induced me
to suppose that we never would be. . . ."

That was the twenty-two-year-old John Bly speaking on
December 5 on the eve of his hanging. With the aid of a
correspondent from the *American Mercury* of Hartford,
which later published his statement, he drew up an address
"To the Good People of Massachusetts," describing his
experience as a Shays man. His gallows companion,
Charles Rose, signed the document, but refused to add
any information about himself. Rose's one hope at this
point was that his friends in England would never learn
the manner of his death.

Bly, a native of Voluntun, Connecticut, had served an

apprenticeship to a tailor in Rhode Island, and had come
to Massachusetts just in time to join the insurrection.
Taken prisoner as a member of Hamlin's party, he had
been discharged by the court, but hearing that new evidence had come up against him, he fled again and lived an
uneasy life on both sides of the New York border. At various times he had raised reinforcements for Shays, made
raids into Stockbridge and Sheffield, once to collect arms,
again to pick up a suit of clothes belonging to a confeder-
ate. It was not until after he heard of Hancock's offer of
pardon that he dared return and settle down. Four weeks
later he was thrown into Great Barrington jail, tried, and
condemned to death.

Having completed his confession, which was rich in
detail and contained one accusation, young Bly opened
the hortatory part of his address.

"Our fate is a loud and solemn lesson to you who have
excited the people to rise against the government . . . .
Remember, we beseech you, that at the final rendering of
judgment you cannot procure your pardon by selecting
men like yourselves to legislate for you. . . . Live peaceably with all men . . . be not too jealous of your rulers
. . . remember that government is absolutely necessary
to restrain the corrupt passions of men. . . . Obey your
honest governors . . . be not allured by designing men.
. . . Pay your honest debts and your reasonable taxes.
. . . Use your utmost endeavors to give peace to your
divided, distracted country." He concluded with an appeal
to "the Son of God, who promised a blessing to the dying
thief."

This warning was addressed not only to the people,
but more specifically to Daniel Shays and to "the selectmen of towns who have been instrumental in raising the
opposition to the government of this commonwealth."

Bly's words, heartfelt though they were, laid insufficient stress on the crime for which he was condemned. The state had not believed his story that he had a right to the suit of clothes he had admitted picking up in the course of a raid on Sheffield. They called it burglary, and that was a crime unpardonable even by John Hancock. The young government's notion of fidelity to the state might be ill-defined, but its conviction of the sacredness of property rights went back to the Pentateuch and to the foundations of the earth.

CHAPTER XX

More Perfect Union

The rebellion was over, at least for the time. In the broader sense it wasn't over at all and perhaps could never be. The principle of rebellion is like chain reaction; or, perhaps better, it is like a seed which once put in the soil may lie dormant until under favorable conditions it puts forth sprout and leaf and bloom and falls only to seed the soil again.

This seed would seldom lie dormant long. The farmers of Pennsylvania in their turn would object to taxes, and there would come what was called the Whisky Rebellion. Some of its phases would be less polite, less restrained than what had gone on under Daniel Shays, gentleman; and Washington, who had not been without sympathy for the Massachusetts insurgents, would be exceedingly wroth. It would come to a disastrous flowering in what Massachusetts would call the Rebellion, and what Washington's Virginia, which achieved a hatred of Boston that made the sentiments of the Shaysites look like sheer affection, called the War between the States.

It would take root in the great West beyond the Berkshires, in fine fat lands still undreamed of in the philosophies of Pelham, and become a hundred movements. Most of the demands of the Shays men would find expression there: the cry for paper money, the protest against taxes, the ancient resentments against the merchants of the East. There would be the Greenback Party, the Grangers, the Populists, Bryan's Cross-of-Gold Speech, the Farmers' Holiday, the rise of that brand of rural statesmanship expressed in the great co-operatives.

Still, there was peace more often than not in Massachusetts. The rebels settled down. Problems, if not solved, were at least ameliorated, in part by the Massachusetts Legislature, in part by a more powerful national government which the rebels themselves unwittingly helped make possible, in part by God Almighty.

In the spring of 1787 the Massachusetts papers, then still full of the commotions, found space for something which looked irrelevant but actually had a vital bearing on the problems of farmers trying to wrench a living from the stony acres of western Massachusetts. They were the advertisements of the Ohio Valley Company. Shays' old commanding officer and good friend General Rufus Putnam was ready at last. While John Hancock and his Council struggled with the question of reprieve or pardon for rebels, Putnam led a caravan from Danvers, the old Salem Village of the Putnam clan, and headed west across the Berkshires, across New York State, still root-bound by the inequities of the patroon system, into the Ohio Valley. There he founded Marietta, and with Marietta the beginnings of a new, larger, more gracious world.

Because the lands were good, and by God's grace illimitable, the farmers there would found a commonwealth closer to the dictates of a farmer's heart. Slavery, thanks to Putnam, would be forbidden, and the more subtle form of slavery suffered by the poor husbandmen and laborers in Massachusetts abolished by universal manhood suffrage. There were to be no "poor polls" in the Ohio

country, and thanks to the influence of what became a
mighty and benign power to the west, there were presently
no more in Joseph Hawley's Massachusetts.

With the opening of the new lands the discontented,
the unlucky, and the restless adventure-seekers of New
England had a place to go. The borders were no longer
sealed up by New York's intransigent management of its
own fat lands; there was hope beyond New York, and
presently in New York itself, whose patroons could not
under the new pressures hold to the feudal code forever.
If some of the adventurers kept their discontent and
found old problems facing them in a new place, more of
them prospered; at least there was respite for all. By
God's providence there was bounty. Some of the fat lands
were already occupied. The men of New England, and for
that matter of the South, could not go west without finding what they wanted already in possession. But the pos-
sessors were only red men, and the peculiar problems of
the Indians are no part of this story.

2.

Another amelioration — or at least transmutation —
of Massachusetts's problems was the adoption of the
Federal Constitution. This was no part of the rebels'
plan; it was carried out against their bitter opposition.
Nevertheless, but for them it might not have come to
pass. They had provided the great object lesson of the dis-
united states. They had shocked George Washington out
of his plans for retirement; they had given Alexander
Hamilton a classic example to be referred to constantly
and with telling effect in his *Federalist* papers. And they
had led their state into the discovery that even the most
proudly sovereign of states is not an island to itself, and
cannot in time of crisis go it alone. Massachusetts had

been humbling itself to ask help of its neighbors; it had been praying to the higher power in Continental Congress and discovering its frailty. "You will not hesitate to adopt . . . a firm, efficient federal government," Newton had instructed its representative.

But Newton wasn't Pelham, or even Worcester, Northampton, or Pittsfield, and Newton wasn't Sam Adams. All of these places and these people were shocked at what had come out of the convention. The members had exceeded their instructions; this was not the "revision" of the Articles of Confederation they had been sent into conclave to achieve. It was a new government. Adopting it would be as revolutionary an act as anything that had happened at Lexington or Concord, or, for that matter, at the Springfield arsenal. More accurately, adopting it would entail a counterrevolution, with the powers of federalism and the presidency substituted for those of Parliament and King George.

"As I enter the building I stumble at the threshold," confessed Sam Adams after scrutinizing this document. "I meet with a national government instead of a federal union of sovereign states. . . . Can this national legislature be competent to make laws for the *free* national government of one people, living in climates so remote, and whose 'habits and partial interests' are and probably always will be so different? . . . May we not look for discontent, mistrust, disaffection to government, and frequent insurrections that will require standing armies to suppress them?"

Shays' Rebellion had filled the old revolutionary with a very human despair. Some of it he let overflow into this letter, which was to his old friend and ally in the Continental Congress, Richard Henry Lee. "So great is the wickedness of some men, and the stupid servility of others that one would be almost inclined to conclude that communities cannot be free. The few haughty families think that they must govern; the body of the people tamely consent and submit to be their slaves."

"Tamely submit." Did this describe Shays or Eli Parsons, who at this writing were beginning the second winter of their exile? It would, could they have known it, have been a golden moment for the remnants of insurgency to join forces with the old patriot of Boston. They couldn't know it. Their ears still rang with his call for the blood of the rebels. And Sam Adams was keeping his dismay very quiet. Lee he might confide in, but Lee was in Virginia; in Boston he moved warily, taking soundings, delaying the public stand that would have given the numerically powerful opposition to the constitution a standard-bearer.

Sam's misgivings were, however, no secret from members of the Federalist Party. They made it their business to prevent his giving them a public utterance which might provide the opposition with a spokesman of prestige. They were aided by Sam's own repugnance to many individual anti-Federalists. Aside from vociferous members from Maine, the majority of such delegates to the convention called in Massachusetts in January 1788 to consider ratification of the constitution were from the insurgent counties, and many had been actual participants in the rebellion.

The Reverend Caleb Curtis, whose prayers had been seditious, was here from Charlton; Phanuel Bishop, who had acted as liaison between county conventions, represented unreconstructed Rehoboth; Josiah Whitney represented Harvard; Samuel Willard, Uxbridge. The representatives from South Brimfield, Shutesbury, and Longmeadow were three of Shays' Committee of Seventeen. Adam Wheeler was rumored to be representing his town, though this was a canard; Wheeler still remained, unforgiven, in Vermont. The disbarred judge William Whiting was fighting for a seat as representative of Great Barrington.

Not easily could Sam Adams have allied himself with such men, many of whom he still considered overdue at the gallows, yet politics is notorious for making strange bedfellows. With a political know-how many of them had learned from Sam himself, the Federalist leaders worked to prevent the unnatural but not impossible alliance.

They considered and rejected the notion of arranging that Sam not be elected to the convention. Exposing him to "such mortification" was too risky, thought Christopher Gore; it might drive him to declare himself openly "and endeavor to make proselytes." Sam was elected, but every precaution was taken to keep him quiet. When Bowdoin planned a dinner party to allow informal discussion of the issues before the convention, he was warned to revise his plans. Sam would be there, would have to be there, but there must not be the kind of table talk that would lead him to commit himself.

To the best of their ability the Federalists packed the convention with men of their own mind. Rufus King was somehow elected delegate from Newburyport, though he hadn't seen the place for years and had to be imported from New York for the purpose. Elbridge Gerry, dissenting member from Massachusetts to the convention which had drawn up the constitution, which he had refused to sign, was in effect excluded from this body.

George Minot, who was for the constitution and against insurgents — he was writing a history of the rebellion — was indignant at the unworthiness of the means used to push so worthy a cause. "Mr. Samuel

Adams was personally insulted," he confided to his diary, "in such a manner as not to admit of his speaking or thinking with freedom. . . ."

Sam had another reason for silence. During the convention he, like Hancock the previous January, had the grief of losing his only son. The convention adjourned a day to attend the funeral. Stoically Sam returned to play his part, but he did little more than watch the creation of a world he personally understood little better than did Daniel Shays.

The nearest he came to speaking his mind was when a Maine delegate expressed impatience to get the convention over with and go home. "I am one of those who have difficulties and doubts respecting some points of the proposed constitution," said Sam. "I have chosen rather to be an auditor than an objector, and I have particular reasons." But he wanted "a full investigation of the subject. . . . We ought not . . . to be stingy of our time or of the public money where so important an object demands them. . . . I am sorry for the gentlemen's necessities, but I'd rather support the gentlemen who are thus necessitated or lend them money to do it, than that they should hurry so great an object."

This outburst caused an excited buzzing in the gallery. Sam, who thought he was being hissed, was ruffled, and hardly spoke again. His strong point had never been oratory but maneuvering behind scenes, and now, watched as he was by masters, he was outmaneuvered. The Federalists engineered the artisans of Boston into taking a public stand for the constitution, and Sam was helpless. "He is too old not to know that his dependence is more on the people than theirs on him," Gore observed.

The delegates from the western counties found their

mouths stopped by the erudition of the Federalists. Only Samuel Willard was learned enough to try to match them on the grounds of classical allusion. He cited the Amphictyonic League as proof that "where power had been trusted to men . . . republics had degenerated into aristocracies." But the Federal classicists snubbed him by the remark that what America was undertaking was without precedent and the Amphictyonic League was irrelevant.

Daddy Singletarry, not an insurgent, but voting with the insurgents, could not long be silenced. He objected to the lack of religious qualification for public office: "We may have an atheist, pagan, Mohammedan." He feared the power vested in the constitution; he resented the eloquence of "these lawyers and men of learning and moneyed men that talk so finely and gloss over matters so smoothly, to make us poor, illiterate people swallow the pill. . . . They expect to be the managers of the constitution . . . and swallow up all us little folks . . . just as the whale swallowed Jonah."

The fight was close. Singletarry's "little people" could not carry their point in debate, but they could vote, and not all the eloquence of a Fisher Ames or a Rufus King could induce them to change their vote. John Hancock, whom they trusted, had absented himself; he was pampering his gout and watching a private scoreboard of his own from his home on Beacon Hill. When at last he took over his duties as president of the convention, he came out for ratification. Sam Adams decided not to desert his old friends, sundry others made up their minds, and the convention was ratified by Massachusetts. And as Massachusetts went, so went the nation.

There was relief after all. The assumption of the state

debts by the new government and Hamilton's funding thereof did in the end bring relief to Massachusetts farmers by making possible a cut in taxes.

3.

"Your petitioners by the melancholy sense of their late errors, and anxious once more to return again to the bosom of their country and enjoy the blessings of peace under the mild operation of its laws, humbly beg leave to supplicate the mercy of the Legislature in their favor."

The petitioners, Daniel Shays and Eli Parsons, were almost the last of the insurgent leaders to be accounted for. Luke Day had fallen into the hands of authority when at sunset of New Year's Day he had incautiously left the sanctuary of Vermont for Westmoreland, New Hampshire. Never one to creep about and travel incognito, he hadn't left the ferry ten minutes before he was in custody. Since then he had been taken to Boston.

The case of William Manning, named in the list of rebels excluded from indemnity, still gave Governor and Council some concern. Apparently he hadn't appreciated the offer to commute a potential death sentence to seven years' hard labor at Castle Island, for Castle Island had seen nothing of him. The offer was in January repeated with a stern note to Sheriff Hyde, expressing surprise at the delay. Reluctantly Manning came to Castle Island and served at least a fraction of his sentence before he was pardoned.

Manning was small potatoes. What the House of Representatives, to whom the petition was addressed, now had on the line was the two archrebels. And this petition was in the proper tone of supplication without overtones of political pressure.

Shays and Parsons no longer justified their conduct;

their penitence, they promised, would be proved by their future behavior. "They will never cease to remember with regret their not having trusted for relief to the wisdom and integrity of the ruling power." Their errors "proceeded from a misapprehension of the facts, from a failure of judgment, and a too precipitate resentment, but by no means from an abandoned principle." They denied that in exile they had ever combined with the enemies of their country. "However criminal they may have been in other respects, they cannot be justly reproached with this enormity."

Punished they had already been. "There is scarcely an inconvenience or misfortune to which they have not already been exposed." If further punishment were deemed necessary, they would not shrink from it, but they wished "to have an opportunity of proving to the world the sincerity of their reform and of adding another instance to those which have been already so conspicuous from the clemency of this Honorable Court."

The petition was read before the House on March 10, 1788, but the mills of the law worked slowly to grind out an answer. The House would have granted it, but the Senate inquired what Shays and Parsons had done to deserve mercy. Nevertheless, steps were taken. On April 2 Hancock withdrew the offer of reward for the return of the rebels, and on the following day sent a copy of his annulment to the other Governors, asking them to follow suit.

In June the situation was reviewed before the Legislature, and a general act of pardon proclaimed. It remained at first conditional, so far as the nine offenders named in Hancock's proclamation of the previous year were concerned; these were forbidden to hold office civil or military. But on June 25 even this disability was removed. Luke Day, after two months' imprisonment in Boston,

had already received pardon by name. How unconditionally civil rights were to be restored in practice remained, nevertheless, in some doubt. In September of
1788 Job Shattuck was denied the privilege of serving on
the Middlesex grand jury. But this "arbitary proceeding"
drew an immediate attack from the *Independent Chronicle*.

Shays returned and took up his life again in Pelham.
But he did not prosper there. The political law might deal
kindly by him, but the harsher economic law did not. The
Massachusetts Centinel heard that he put some time in
debtors' prison in 1792. Perhaps he still owed for the en-
tertainment he had given his general staff in 1787.

Presently he too joined the surge of movement to the
west. He did not venture as far as Rufus Putnam, but settled in a newfound village in central New York whose
name, which was Sparta, should have pleased Sam Adams.
At first he was a mere squatter, less of a reproach in a
place where land titles were harder to come by than elsewhere. He had come alone (what had become of his Abigail, who had followed him loyally into his exile in Vermont?) and had the good fortune to please a woman with
a modest estate of her own. The widow of Darling
Havens, who had been a tavernkeeper, became his wife,
and he lived out his days with her.

There was nothing of the rebel in the aging Shays, now
chiefly interested in keeping the pension he received from
the government as a veteran of the Revolution. He would
have been as shocked as was Boston at Sam Adams, who,
becoming Governor of Massachusetts after the death of
John Hancock, had unexpectedly turned revolutionary
again, at least to the extent of applauding certain subversive activities in France.

Shays' career, however, had not been altogether forgotten. Sometimes travelers came to look him up, exactly as wayfarers in Virginia stopped off at Mount Vernon for a look at its celebrated squire. One of them, a future President of the United States, young Millard Fillmore, was disappointed in what he found. Shays had become an old man like any other, a bit too fond of the bottle, they said in Sparta, but not one to frequent low places or keep low company. In spite of his slender means, he set a good table and entertained graciously. But there was nothing about him to suggest the legendary figure that had caused the hills of Berkshire to ring with the cry "Hurrah for Daniel Shays!"

He was fourscore-four when he died in 1825, and by then such was his obscurity and his poverty that no one troubled to put a marker on his grave. Even the name of Sparta, his adopted town, has vanished from the map; his grave must be sought for in Conesus.

There are more proper memorials in his native state. Springfield has honored with a tablet his attempt to get into the arsenal. On the wind-swept summit of East Hill in Pelham, on the Daniel Shays Highway, outside the little white meetinghouse that Shays knew so well, there is another, praising his attempts to oppose "unjust laws." Perhaps perversely, perhaps quite reasonably, Massachusetts has grown proud of him.

4.

"Let the evening of his life be made pleasant by a reward of his faithfulness; then will you prove yourselves the rewarder of faithful worth and evidence to the world that you have not forgot THE MAN who so skillfully assisted in rearing the first cellar of our independence."

It was a writer in the *Independent Chronicle* in 1788 advocating the election of Sam Adams as Lieutenant

Governor. The plea, which somehow implied that the post
was a sentimental souvenir to be handed out as an award
of merit, was not entirely flattering either to Massachusetts or to Sam.

He didn't get it, not in a year when Shays was still an
issue. But a year later, when Shays and everyone else had
been safely pardoned and the old ringleaders of the rebellion of 1775 were warm friends again, Hancock's efforts
got Sam Adams elected as Lieutenant Governor. And in
1793, when Hancock died in office of an affliction which
never seemed "marvelous" to him, Sam succeeded to first
honors in his commonwealth. He became Governor in his
own right in 1794, and remained in office until of his own
accord he retired two years later. To the last he stoutly
tried to turn back the tides of modernism from Boston
and shape it to his own ideal of the Christian Sparta.

In office he was what he had not been as member of the
Senate, a revolutionary again. Rebellion had broken out
in Lafayette's France. Its details speedily scandalized the
more proper Bostonians, but not the mechanics, who
were organizing Jacobin Clubs and learning to sing *"Ça
Ira,"* and, above all, not Sam Adams.

Quite as shocking to Boston as the excesses of the
French was the spectacle of a Governor who continued
to applaud whatever the French did at a time when any
expression of approval counted as subversive activity. Nor
was Adams's applause reserved only for a revolution
far away; there was in Boston a riot that terrorized the
property-holders for six days, and Adams gave evidence
of positively enjoying the commotions. "It's only a water-
melon riot," he said when even his Betsy appealed to him
to stop it.

It was well that Sam craved the sweets of retirement
when he did; he would have tasted them in any case. He

settled down in his shabby house on Winter Street and made again a virtue of Spartan frugality. This was now by choice, not necessity. Like Daniel Shays, he had come by a pension, his son's. He invested it with an acumen unprecedented in his branch of the Adams family, largely in real estate in the flourishing suburb of Jamaica Plains, and died in comfortable circumstances.

His grave is not unmarked. In fact, there is in Boston no stone more publicly placed. From his grave just off the sidewalks of Tremont Street, Sam Adams watches over the destinies of his beloved Boston, a government which, as Eli Parsons would have it, changes with the changing times.

A NOTE ON SOURCES

My own method of undertaking long-range research is to get the general facts well in hand from the secondary sources before taking on the labyrinthine documents. Following this rule, I approached Shays' Rebellion by way of George Richard Minot's *History of the Insurrections in Massachusetts,* written in 1788 while the rebellion was still news, and Josiah Gilbert Holland's *History of Western Massachusetts* (Springfield, 1855).

Along the way I also made use of Joseph Parker Warren's *The Shays Rebellion,* a doctor's dissertation still in the manuscript at the Widener Library, Anson Ely Morse's very helpful *Federalist Party in Massachusetts to the Year 1800* (Princeton, 1909), and, though necessarily I came to it belatedly, Robert J. Taylor's *Western Massachusetts in the Revolution* (Brown University, 1954).

The most indispensable primary sources on the rebellion are the six massive volumes of documents in the Massachusetts Archives, the ones numbered 189, 190, 191, 192, 318, 319. These I studied in detail, returning to them again and again as collateral research gave me fresh insights into initially obscure situations. I also explored in the Archives many accessory volumes of correspondence, resolutions, the journals of House and Senate, and the especially significant material in Volume 30, which contains the deliberations of the Governor's Council during this period.

I found what seemed to be a virgin field in the Records of the Massachusetts Supreme Judicial Court in the Suffolk County Courthouse in Boston. The arrangement is baffling; there is an index, but to use it one must know the name of the culprit, the approximate date of his crime, and the county in which he committed it. Running down any given subject, however, is often rewarded by

255

the discovery of a wealth of cognate material in the same box. For the aid of future students of Shays' Rebellion I offer two numbers: look for the testimony on the "rebel" judge, William Whiting, in 160304; for Perez Hamlin, Berkshire leader, in 160538.

The Massachusetts Historical Society has many documents of interest. The Knox Manuscripts, XIX, XX, contain dozens of sidelights on the rebellion, including Henry Knox's reminder to Lafayette that Shays had once served under his command. The Robert Treat Paine papers include one small but meaty volume on events in Hampshire and Worcester counties. Of the voluminous Theodore Sedgwick papers, the relevant collections are Boxes A, and 1 and 3; they include a journal kept in the winter campaign by a member of General Benjamin Lincoln's staff, and a brief, highly opinionated diary by Minot, first historian of the rebellion. (Sedgwick's own letters on the rebellion are in the Massachusetts Archives.)

In Northampton, I looked into the records of the Court of Common Pleas in the Courthouse, and the Judd Manuscripts, especially the diaries of the Jonathan Judds, father and son, at the Forbes Library. I also had the pleasure of examining Sidney Kaplan's enormous private collection of notes, and the satisfaction of finding the old jail and debtors'-prison records at the House of Correction. Here is the record of Luke Day's term in debtors' prison, and accounts of men jailed in Hampshire County during the rebellion.

I found Shays' army record in the National Archives in Washington, and much incidental background material in the Manuscript Room of the New York Public Library; my investigations included the Hawley Papers, the Samuel Adams Papers, and the records of the Committees of Correspondence.

Refreshingly uninhibited views of the rebellion are to be found among the Royall Tyler Collection at the Vermont Historical Society at Montpelier, Vermont. Most of the Vermont phase of Shays' adventures is based on this material as supplemented by Tyler's more official reports in the Massachusetts Archives.

I made a careful study of the files of five newspapers printed during the rebellion years. They were the *Hampshire Gazette* (Northampton); the *Independent Chronicle* and the *Massachusetts Cen-*

tinel (Boston); and the *Massachusetts Spy* and the *Worcester Magazine* (Worcester). Properly the two latter, both edited by Isaiah Thomas, are the same; the one suspended publication and became a "magazine" in 1786 to escape the imposition of the "Stamp Act."

Though I am indebted for much good material to these papers, I must say that I found eighteenth-century journalism exasperating; so much space was given to Ciceronian eloquence, and so little to homely detail. This, I might add, is a trait that runs through many of the documents; every man alive in that period, from G. Washington to D. Shays, seemed bent on rounding off periods of neo-classical elegance, though Shays, whose natural idiom apparently ran to phrases like "I wa'n't got there then," usually left an artless participle dangling.

I owe much to printed collections, including notably the Bowdoin-Temple Papers, the Belknap Papers, and the Warren-Adams Letters, all published by the Massachusetts Historical Society. I bless the *New England Historical and Genealogical Register* for publishing the diary of James Parker (1915, Mrs. Ethel Stanwood, editor). To this mine of rural folkways of the 1780's I returned constantly. In its different way, William Pyncheon's diary, edited by Fitch Edward Oliver (1890), offered useful material. My material for the convention called in Massachusetts to ratify the Constitution came from an unexpectedly flavorful book published by the state in 1856 under the title of *Debates and Proceedings*.

Many lives and memoirs of notables of the period were helpful, notably Thomas C. Amory's *Life of James Sullivan* (Boston, 1859); Charles R. King's *Life and Correspondence of Rufus King* (New York, 1894); Rufus Putnam's *Memoirs* (Cambridge, 1903); William Sullivan's *Familiar Letters* (Boston, 1834); the last was especially valuable in that Sullivan wrote not only of what people did, but how they looked doing it.

Of the scores of town histories I ransacked, I owe most to Mason A. Green's *Springfield* (Boston, 1888); Mabel Cook Coolidge's *History of Petersham* (Hudson, 1948); C. O. Parmenter's *History of Pelham, Massachusetts* (Amherst, 1898); J. E. A.

Smith's *History of Pittsfield, Massachusetts* (Boston, 1869);
James Russell Trumbull's *History of Northampton* (Northampton, 1902).

In this category also belong Timothy Dwight's four-volume
Travels in New England and New York (New Haven, 1821–2),
useful because he gave attention to the appearance of the towns he
visited; Thomas Anburey's *Travels through Interior Parts of
America* (Boston, 1923), which contains graphic material on how
up-country Americans looked to a chivalric young Englishman;
Samuel Deane's *New England Farmer* (Worcester, 1790), a mine
of information about New England husbandry; Jedidiah Morse's
The American Geography (Elizabethtown, New Jersey, 1789),
which includes some direct reporting on the rebellion.

Many books were of value in obtaining and correcting perspective, among them Merrill Jensen's *The New Nation, a History of
the United States during the Confederation 1781–1798* (New
York, 1950); Carl C. Taylor's *The Farmer's Movement, 1620–
1920* (New York, 1953); J. Franklin Jameson's *The American
Revolution Considered as a Social Movement* (Princeton, 1926).

Except for Edward Bellamy's *Duke of Stockbridge* (New York,
1900), I kept away from the several fictional works of the rebellion. Bellamy's value to me lay in his intimate knowledge of
Berkshire backgrounds; his story of the "Duke" (Perez Hamlin)
is romantic fiction; a glance into the records of the Massachusetts
Supreme Judicial Court would have ruined his story for him, and
since it's a good story, it's just as well he didn't look.

INDEX

[All towns listed are in Massachusetts unless otherwise noted.]

i

A NOTE ON THE TYPE

This book is set in Linotype CASLON, a modern adaptation of a type designed by the first William Caslon (1692–1766). The Caslon face has had two centuries of ever-increasing popularity in the United States — it is of interest to note that the first copies of the Declaration of Independence and the first paper currency distributed to the citizens of the new-born nation were printed in this type face.

Composed, printed, and bound by Kingsport Press, Inc., Kingsport, Tenn. Paper made by P. H. Glatfelter Co., Spring Grove, Pa.

D